MACHINE
THAT RUNS THE WORLD

MACHINE
THAT RUNS THE WORLD

SYED NASER MOHIUDDIN

www.whitefalconpublishing.com

Machine that Runs the World
Syed Naser Mohiuddin

www.whitefalconpublishing.com

All rights reserved
First Edition, 2022
© Syed Naser Mohiuddin, 2022
Cover design by White Falcon Publishing, 2022
Cover image source freepik.com

No part of this publication may be reproduced, or stored in a retrieval system, or transmitted in any form by means of electronic, mechanical, photocopying or otherwise, without prior written permission from the author.

The contents of this book have been certified and timestamped on the POA Network blockchain as a permanent proof of existence. Scan the QR code or visit the URL given on the back cover to verify the blockchain certification for this book.

The views expressed in this work are solely those of the author and do not reflect the views of the publisher, and the publisher hereby disclaims any responsibility for them.

Requests for permission should be addressed to
economics.machine@gmail.com

ISBN - 978-1-63640-652-7

Care has been taken to ensure accuracy of the information provided in this book in good faith, however, neither the author nor the publisher have a liability to the consumer of this book for any loss or damage of any kind incurred on account of use of the information. All the information provided in this book is without guarantee on part of the author or publisher. In addition, the publisher and the author assume no responsibility for errors, inaccuracies, omissions, or any other inconsistencies herein.

In case any user finds a factual error in the book, we would be thankful if they let us know on economics.machine@gmail.com, which we would attempt to correct in subsequent editions.

Contents

Part – I Macroeconomics

1. Evolution of Money and Central Banks 3
2. The Idea Called GDP 10
3. "Inflation" - Not an Irrelevant Arcane Metric 17
4. Basics of Business of Banking.. 22
5. Return on Capital vs. Return on Labor - How is It Related to Your Personal Wealth 32
6. Exports vs. Imports: A Tussle Involving Economics as Well as Politics...38
7. Impact of State and Mega Firms on Individual Prosperity 44
8. Opportunities and Trends in the Next Wave of Progress..51
9. Lessons from Economic Disasters......................................76
10. Shape and Form of Different Industries 96

Contents

Part – II Business Management, Finance and Company Operations

11 Introduction to Financial Statements 105

12 Accounting Discretion Available in Financial Statements 112

13 Cash Management..118

14 Financial Ratios – The Tools for Benchmarking Business Performance 123

15 Cost at Which Companies Obtain Money......................132

16 Company Valuations – Simplified 135

17 Investing in Stocks..142

18 Costing 147

19 A Few Pointers for Start Ups 151

Conclusion 159

Reading Resources 161

References 163

Preface

The act of voluntarily exchanging stuff, in mutually agreed quantities, between two humans is probably as old as mankind itself. This act, which, by definition, is trading, precedes culture, society and governance. This ability to exchange excess of any good with another person resulted in the benefit of both parties involved, created abundance for either of them and provided them excess time that they eventually utilized for things like storytelling, culture and art. It is probably for this reason that Maynard Keynes has remarked about economists that they are the trustees not of the civilization, but the possibility of civilization.[1] So, it is no exaggeration to say that understanding the basics of economics is a prerequisite for a civilized mind. But the era of specialization has narrowed the working ground of every individual and, like many other basic human skills, understanding of trade and economics has been relegated to an insignificant corner of life. And inclination of economists to define their theories in the form of mathematical equations has only catalyzed this neglect!

While we were busy *not* understanding economics and business, their importance grew in our lives without us noticing. Understanding economics can help in individual prosperity as well as collective abundance of societies. Individuals who understand economics and business can make an extraordinary contribution to mankind through enterprise at a personal level and right questioning at a collective level. Most of the countries across the world are democracies. Politicians running these democracies passively and actively respond to the kind of questions the citizenry asks them. Thus, awareness and basic understanding of matters of governance, of which economics is a vital component, is very important since the right kind of questioning improves our collective lives as well as abates our individual progress.

Speaking of individual progress, previously, we humans used to keep score of our rat race of life on multiple metrics, like knowledge, spirituality, chivalry, bravery, physical strength and prosperity. But, today, prosperity takes lion's share of the pie to define our self-worth and success. Understanding economics is not just about educating ourselves for sake of the "possibility of civilization", it is equally important for the sake of success as we have come to define it.

Closing sentences of Thomas Piketty's book *Capital in Twenty-First Century* would be the best way to drive the point home. He pointed out that everyone, regardless of their background, should take a serious interest in money, its measurement, the facts surrounding it and its history. It is because refusing to deal with numbers and money rarely serves one's interests.

This book is an attempt to demystify economics to all citizens in general and those who are trying a hand at business management in particular; an attempt at understanding how money can be deployed, how its measurement is kept, the facts

Preface

surrounding it, its history and, most importantly, an attempt at understanding how it can be increased. The book proposes no new theory; rather it cites and presents generally available economic and business ideas and tones them down for mass consumption.

***

Introduction

An attempt has been made to keep the book simple and relatable and an earnest effort has been made to keep the equations at bay. It is a book by an amateur attempting to demystify different economic theories, functioning of monetary and taxation policies, companies and industries so that economics, business and investing become relatively palatable.

If you ever wondered what exactly 'inflation' means and how does it benefits or harms you when it rises/falls, this book is probably for you. If you are a middle-level manager with no formal business education and would like to skill yourself up so that you can better read a balance sheet or be in better control when financial jargon is being jettisoned around in corporate meetings, this book is probably for you. It is a book that attempts to spread the 'gospel of amateur economics'. It is meant to identify the elements of economics and review their structure.

Economics narrates our constant move towards specialization as producers and diversification as consumers. And this move is influenced by resources, opportunities, rule of law, geography, ideology, institutions and luck. Economics attempts to explain how humans transact as they respond

Introduction

collectively and individually to these influences. In other words, it probes at both micro and macro levels. To mimic this classification, this book as well is divided into two parts:

1. Macroeconomics and functioning of industries
2. Business management

The first part is focused on a wider audience and attempts to cover subjects of economics and its effects on individuals. The second part is primarily focused on the demystification of the elements and the aspects of managing a firm – the bunch of micro-skills that might help you develop expertise in business management. The latter part might be of higher interest to those who are running firms or those who intend to run firms.

Part – I

Macroeconomics

1

Evolution of Money and Central Banks

How are economy and circulation of currency related? How do banks influence demand and production in an economy? To understand the answers to these questions, let us begin with understanding what money exactly is!

A well-functioning money circulation system is a prerequisite to a prospering and functioning civilization. Money helps people in fixing the values of articles they want to obtain and get rid of. The amount of money in a country should keep pace with the size and mix of its economic activity; too much money would end its relevance with the real economy (one can read about the German inflation of 1930) and too less of it would turn into a constraint on transactions.

Evolution of Currency as We Know It:

At the beginning of society, when humans initiated transacting through the barter system, they faced the primary issue of "inconvenience". You needed to find someone who not only has what you need but also wants what you have!! This problem of bi-directional match-making made people use grains as an exchange currency since almost everybody needed grains to survive. However, as the economy started growing, the next requirement was that the currency should not just be a medium of exchange of value, but also should be a medium of store of value. You have to store your wealth. Grains were relatively temporary. They could rot. Maybe seashells were a good alternative! They became the medium of exchange in some of the primitive societies. And, it has to be kept in mind that not every seashell was used as currency. But then, a problem emerged. Circulation of seashells increased as they were being picked up from beaches, but a lot of seashells were chasing the same goods and services available in the economy. They lost their value (it was essentially inflation due to the circulation of more than the required currency, the kind that was faced by Germany in 1930).

People needed something that is not so easily available as seashells and is more permanent than grain. They chose metals! Having any metal as a currency could land the system into the same problem as that faced while using seashells. Thus, gold and silver became the "gold standard" of wealth - they were relatively permanent and were rare enough that they didn't lose their value. They could be used as a store of value. Things went on fine for quite a few centuries when gold and silver coins were essentially the store of value for almost the whole of the civilized world. Since the metal was heavy and difficult to carry around, people stored those gold coins in banks and banks gave a promissory "note" saying "I promise to pay the bearer of this note so and so the amount of gold". Thus, "bank notes" became the next currency. Things went fine all through medieval times till the beginning of the 20th century.

But using gold/silver as an exchange of wealth had an inherent flaw! Suppose a country's economy is growing at, say, 5% in a given year, but the amount of new gold being dug/acquired by that country has only a 3% growth rate, the

1 Evolution of Money and Central Banks

currency (either gold coins or "bank notes" attached to those gold coins) will become a hindrance to economy. People need around 5% more coins to run their affairs but they got only 3% more!! This issue will lead to "deflation": Less money chasing more goods and services, leading to goods and services becoming cheaper day by day. (You will get a car for 500 gm of gold, which previously was for 600 gm of gold because there is no gold in the economy but the carmaker wants to sell off the cars that are waiting in his/her warehouse). This would, in turn, be a disincentive for producers (they don't want to sell cheaper goods), and also, people would stop buying, hoping that things will become cheaper. This will lead to the economy coming to a standstill.

The problem could be the other way round too. Too much gold and silver compared to the economy will make them meet the same fate of.... yeah..... seashells. This is what happened during 16th century Europe, when Europeans started bringing hordes of silver mined from Americas.

So, eventually, governments decided to de-link their currency from gold and instead used a set of economic indicators to decide how much currency to print. Gold has arguably stopped being a store of wealth though it is still used as an indicator of wealth.

But governments couldn't print as much money as they wanted to, otherwise, the "notes" printed would essentially meet the same fate as..... yeah you got it right... seashells!! So, irrespective of its form and shape, money survives on the trust in its issuer. If the issuer (in most cases government) abuses their power to issue money, chances are that it would lose its value.

By now it is clear that to be considered a currency, something need not have an inherent consumption value.

It is sufficient to be considered a currency if it can be stored, exchanged, divided and is being accepted by the person with whom you are transacting. Anecdotes of tobacco as a currency in prisons can drive this point home!

Trust in the issuer is a prerequisite for a functioning money system. The banknotes of early banking systems weren't sovereign money (money issued by the government), but they were still being used as a medium of exchange of value since traders trusted banks. At this point, it would be interesting to compare banknotes with cryptocurrencies. They aren't much different from primitive banknotes in this sense. Cryptocurrencies are not government-backed, but they acquired the role of medium of exchange because they were able to fulfill the requirement of 'trust in its issuer'.

Consider the example of Bitcoin, which is one of the most popular cryptocurrencies[1] as of 2020. It is not issued by any sovereign government but is used as a medium of exchange and avenue of investment. The reason is that Bitcoin has decentralized checks and balances to track the transactions and also needs high computing effort to mine (equivalent to minting) new coins. There is also a limit of 21 million on the maximum number of Bitcoins that can ever be produced [2] thus avoiding its value collapse due to coins' proliferation. In fact, a few sovereign governments have begun to accept Bitcoin as a legal tender. El Salvador was the first country to do so.[3]

Role of money in greasing economy:

Money is to the economy what blood is to the human body. Without blood, the energy, the oxygen and the nutrients will not reach the points where they are needed. In the same way,

1 Evolution of Money and Central Banks

when there is a money crunch in an economy, with all its muscles in place, the economy will not be able to get things around!!!

The heart pumps faster when a heavy physical activity is done, the same way the central bank of any country calibrates its circulation of money whenever there is a heavy/diminished economic activity.

Usually heavy supply of money is needed in two situations:

1. When the economy is growing really fast: In such a situation, there would be heavy investments going all around, with the government investing in new infrastructure, businesses investing in new capacity and human resources and individuals buying new stuff with new-found jobs and transactions. In such a situation, the central bank ensures that the liquidity in the system (currency and other immediately convertible forms of wealth) is growing more or less at the same pace as the overall economy, so that the transactions remain well-greased. So, in our "blood" analogy, this is the situation when someone is running really fast and his/her heart is pumping blood at a pace that caters to this speed.
2. When the economy is facing a recession: In such a situation, all the "savers" start withdrawing their money from financial instruments (bank accounts, mutual funds, shares, bonds, etc). Though there is no rise in economic activity, there is a heavy need for cash. If central banks don't supply cash in such situations, banks would not be able to supply the money to those who are withdrawing. This will create further panic and loss of trust in banks and thus cause a lot of damage. So, again, in our "blood" analogy, this is akin to a situation where

though there is no heavy physical activity, there is a shortage of blood and such a situation calls for a "blood transfusion".

In a nutshell, any Central Bank has the task of estimating the amount of liquidity that is needed based on prevailing levels of economic activity. With economic transactions growing more complex and numerous, making this accurate estimation is no small task!! In his book, "The End of Alchemy: Money, Banking and the Future of the Global Economy", Mervyn King, an ex-governor of the Bank of England, narrated an interesting anecdote. In earlier days, the direction and speed of wind used to add to the uncertainty of the arrival times of the ships carrying imports to London, which, in turn, used to add to uncertainty to the cash needed in the market. To cope with these uncertainties, the Court Room of Bank of England had a wind dial fixed to predict the cash needs.[4] So, during those days, it was about winds literally blowing in the right direction! But now, things aren't about having a single dial in the central bank that can accurately predict how many notes should be printed next week!!!! Having understood money, let us now understand the functioning of central banks.

Central Banks:

Central banks, in their basic form, are similar to other banks but have a few additional privileges that are not enjoyed by common banks. The most prominent of the privileges is that they are the only entity in a given country that can print money. In modern economies, central banks perform the task of ensuring the "relevance of amount of currency with the economy". Every other task that central banks perform

1 Evolution of Money and Central Banks

is an offshoot of this primary task. How do central banks pump money into the economy? They purchase government bonds ("I owe you" slips by the government), print and give the corresponding amount of money to the government. Thus, they create money essentially out of thin air. They get some interest on that money that they gave as a loan to the government and that interest is their income.

Central banks also influence other banks and the amount of money circulating, by altering the rate at which they could lend/borrow from them. Imagine that central bank increases its interest rate. Other banks too adjust their interest rate upward (though not always) and thus people deposit their money in banks instead of spending since they are getting more interest out of it. It plays exactly the other way round if they reduce the interest rate. Thus, increased interest rates suck money out of the economy and decreased rates push money into the hands of people. Thus, whenever the economy is slowing down, apart from the other levers that government uses, the central banks are expected to have a "rate cut" to boost it. Thus, demand and supply are influenced by banks as well, not just by the industry! It is important to note that central banks are 'bankers to banks'. In normal circumstances, the general public doesn't get to interact with central banks.

Having covered money, let us now move to GDP, the metric that is considered a prime economic indicator for most governments.

2

The Idea Called GDP

How do you know if your neighbor is doing fine economically? You estimate his/her economic condition by the car s/he has purchased, by the amount s/he spent on house refurbishment and by the kind of parties s/he is throwing!

Estimating the economic condition of a country is not much different. You estimate how well a country is doing by adding the amount of money that a country has spent and call it GDP. Let us glance through what all goes into GDP (for neighbors, it is car, house, clothes and parties).

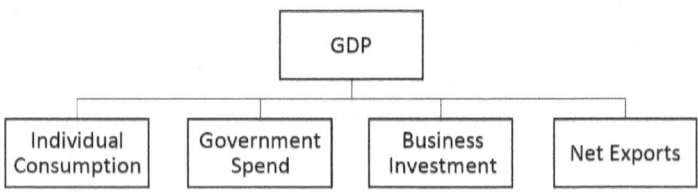

As depicted in the figure above, all the expenses of a country (an economy) are classified into consumption by individuals, government expenditure (for infra and for its day-to-day affairs), business investment and exports.

2 The Idea Called GDP

GDP is a financial estimate of progress - Reasonably acceptable but not highly precise:

The first point to understand about GDP is that it is an estimate in terms of money without any consideration of social/environmental impact or quality of the expenditure.

Here is the explanation: For example, my one-year-old is contributing to GDP in ways in which I wasn't able to! Whenever he refuses to use the potty, we have to spend on a disposable diaper worth $0.2/piece :-) which indeed is a $0.2 contribution to GDP. My mom says she rarely used a disposable diaper for me and thus I didn't get this chance of contributing to GDP :-) :-). Similarly, say, I go swimming and contribute to GDP by buying a membership of the swimming pool, but my dad couldn't do so when he was young, since he used to swim in a neighborhood pond. The above two scenarios are examples where no real "development" happened but GDP grew. Then there would be cases, where real development happened but the GDP didn't grow. For example, suppose there is a medicine that got cheaper after going off-patent. Now more people have access to it and they are spending less on it, but it would look like a loss to GDP since the expenditure by people has reduced. Similarly, consider that there were mineral deposits that a country discovered and started using them in, say, 2020. Its GDP will get impacted by that deposit only from 2020 though the minerals and their associated wealth always existed for use.

The second point is that there is an inherent difficulty associated with the collection and processing of data to estimate a big number like GDP. Similar to how you might make mistakes in assessing the prosperity of your neighbor due to a lack of precise information related to their expenditure, there are many transactions that cannot be/are not baked in GDP due to their sheer size and time-lapse between execution and data compilation. Many informal transactions occur but are not reported/under-reported (would you be able to record the exact price at which vegetables were sold at every single grocery store/pushcart throughout a country in the last year?). So, there is always an element of estimate and 'informal economy' that couldn't be precisely captured in GDP.

Understanding the components of GDP:

The slump or increase in the economic activity is thus indicated (not reflected) by the rise/slowdown of GDP. To enhance the overall economy, the country, as a whole, tries to maximize the "components" of GDP. But each component, by virtue of its nature, needs different impetus, has different causes and impacts, takes different reaction times to respond and has different sets of benefactors. The table below is an attempt at explanation:

	Individual Consumption	Government Expenditure	Business Investment	Net Exports
Income source	Personal income	Direct and indirect taxes	Investment from individuals and profits reinvested	
Purpose of credit	Usually for long-term needs, e.g. home purchase and for milestones of life (education, etc.)	To bridge the gap between income generated by taxes and government expenditure	• For creating new production capacity (plants) • For running day-to-day affairs (called working capital loan)	

2 The Idea Called GDP

Mix of expenditure	Usually short-term; Long-term expenditures include real estate, white goods or automobile	Managing day-to-day affairs of bureaucracy and long-term infra expenditure like roads, rails, power, etc.	Mid-term with a view to generating profits	Dependent upon the condition of international markets
Remarks	• Ease of loans and availability of opportunities and income define expenditure	• Used sometimes to kickstart the business cycle when it has dropped dead! • Government expenditure creates an ecosystem as well as confidence for businesses	• Highly dependent upon purchasing capability and market size of government and individuals	• Linked to business health and investment • Usually a smaller component of the overall GDP

How components of GDP are interlinked?

Imagine that a country, to increase its GDP, increases its government's expenditure. The source of income for such an increase would be either taxes or government bonds (loans from public and central banks).

Increased taxes would reduce the amount of money in the hands of individuals, which, in turn, would reduce the "individual expenditure" component of the GDP and thus would end up curtailing the GDP. This reduced expenditure might impact the revenue being generated by business firms, which, in turn, would reduce the taxes for the government! This can turn into a vicious circle. The correct balance of taxes, government expenditure and individual expenditure is an iterative act of incremental course corrections and fine balance.

Part – I: Macroeconomics

Financial levers that governments pull

To achieve this fine balance, governments pull many levers. Out of those, two are financial levers. One is called fiscal policy and the other one is called monetary policy.

The first lever, fiscal policy, is all about setting the amount of taxation. It covers both direct taxes (income tax and corporate tax) and indirect taxes (sales taxes, GST, customs, etc.). As discussed in the previous paragraph, the government has to be careful, incremental and iterative to ensure that fiscal policy is set just right to ensure the overall welfare of the society. Fiscal policy is impacted by politics, overall situation, maturity of various industries and state's execution capacity. For example, a country with rudimentary government machinery usually has customs as a bigger component of its overall revenue.[1] This is probably because imposing taxes that are entering physical borders is practically easier than, say, taxing internal transactions in an informal economy.

Monetary policy, the second financial lever, is basically the policy around deciding the amount of money circulating in the economy. This is done via central banks in two ways.

1. **By adjusting the interest rates:** The central bank sets an interest rate and banks consider this interest rate to set their own rates that they offer to their depositors. If the central bank's rate is high, banks too set high rates and more people come to banks to deposit their money. If the interest rate is reduced, people tend NOT to deposit their money in banks and they spend it rather than hoard it, thus bringing liquidity to the economy and pushing expenditure.

2 The Idea Called GDP

2. **By altering the amount of currency circulating in the market:** When the government needs to spend, they sell "sovereign bonds". These are basically IOU slips!! The central bank purchases (takes) these IOU slips and gives currency to the government (Theoretically, the central bank has an unlimited capability of printing money). The government takes this currency and spends. Thus, new currency enters the economy.

The monetary policy, too, is about a fine balance between the actual economy and currency. The functioning of central banks discussed in previous chapter has touched upon how this fine balance is achieved.

The other (non-financial) levers to ensure efficient production and thus better GDP growth are stable governance, investor-friendly policies, rule of law (businesses should not be scared that government can take over their firms overnight with some ordinance) and relative ease of initiating and sustaining business (one should not spend months together just to get their work permit).

In conclusion, it is important to repeat the point that was touched upon at the beginning of the chapter. GDP should be taken with a pinch of salt. A hyper-focus on growth has spotlighted GDP more than any other metric. But it should be noted that borders marking the distribution of economic prosperity need not always sync with geographic and political borders. All the segments of society in a country need not be prospering if a country's GDP is growing. Countries should incorporate a few more measures along with GDP to keep a track of their performance.

To begin with, a simple measure around income distribution between different strata of society indicating how national wealth is being produced and being appropriated by different members of the society can be a relief from the extreme focus on GDP. Thomas Piketty, in his book 'Capital and Ideology', proposed an annual measurement of the share of total income or wealth accruing to the bottom 50 percent, the middle 40 percent, and the top 10 percent in each country.[2] Human Development Index initiated by Amartya Sen, which considers three aspects of access to health, education and goods is yet another big attempt to free the macroeconomics measurement from the shackles of GDP.

Having touched on a broad metric that measures overall wealth, let us now cover 'inflation' in the next chapter. It is a measure that influences your expenditure.

3

"Inflation" - Not an Irrelevant Arcane Metric

Inflation is a term that we encounter in news headlines quite often but consider irrelevant for our personal finances. But it deeply influences our progress between economic stations of life. This write-up is an attempt to explain how inflation is defined and how is it deeply related to the man (and woman) on street.

Inflation is rather intuitive. Most of us experience it when we recall how a particular car is still beyond our reach, though our salary has doubled in the last 10 years. But how is it measured? What does the measurement mean? Who benefits from it: the savers or the borrowers? How do we tackle it so that we get better off with passing time and not worse off? Since it is so deeply related to us, we should also understand which government policies affect it the most.

The Idea of Inflation

Consider a person, who has only three basic needs - food, shelter and clothing. And to simplify, let us believe that the person consumes only one type of food, one type of shelter and one type of clothing. For this hypothetically austere person, it would be easy to keep a tab on how his/

her expenses have increased. Imagine that in a year, the expenses of the given person have increased from $100 to $110. We would be able to say that the cost of living for the person has inflated by 10%. In other words, his/her personal inflation is 10%.

But imagine a person, who, like any normal person, keeps altering their consumption of food, clothing and shelter. How would s/he measure the rise in costs? Every few days, s/he would be required to compare the cost of the things that s/he didn't buy last year but is buying this year. It would be pretty confusing! Now extrapolate this for the entire nation, it would be almost impossible!!!

To overcome this impossibility, the government comes up with an "index". The index picks up a spectrum of products and services that the government feels best represents the consumption bucket of its citizens and tracks it year on year. The government keeps updating this list every now and then.

For example, in 2014, the Office of National Statistics in the UK removed DVD recorders and gardener's fees from the Consumer Price Index and replaced them with films streamed over the Internet and fresh fruit snacking pots.[1] The fact that gardener's fees survived in the index till 2014 should make all those who don't have a garden realize that inflation is an indicative number and should be contextualized to our own case if we want to spend right and be better off with passing years.

Having understood that inflation is an indicator of increasing prices, let us ask the question - wouldn't it be a wonderful world if the prices fall rather than rise? No, it wouldn't. The next paragraph explains why it is so!

3 "Inflation" - Not an Irrelevant Arcane Metric

Why Do Prices Rise in the First Place and Why Deflation is Still Worse

Prices increase when the demand is more than the supply. Suppose all the people in a city, put together, want 100 apples. But there are only 95 apples to be sold. Given the fact that the demand is higher and the supply is lesser, the apple trader "slightly" increases the price, and still, people buy those apples. This is the usual cause of inflation. But if the number of apples required is just 50 and there are 100 available, the price would fall. This would be deflation. This, inturn, compels the trader to shut their shop, since s/he would be losing rather than making a profit on their economic activity. Also, people start to postpone their purchases, hoping that the price would further fall. This, in turn, would bring the whole economic activity to a grinding halt. That is why falling prices on a mass scale are bad for the economics of a country.

Low inflation in the range of about 1-2% is good for the economy and is a partial indicator of a near balance between demand and supply.

Demand-supply mismatch is one of the reasons for inflation. The second, scarier reason for inflation is the pumping of currency by the government. Imagine that a government starts printing as much currency as they wish. A lot of money would be chasing the same goods and services. Since a lot of cash is floating around, all the people would come to the shop to purchase those 95 apples and thus shopkeeper would increase the price as much as s/he want. This type of inflation was faced by Germany around 1921-24. In basic terms, this is what happened: the government took a loan from people (in form of government bonds) for funding the war, and since it de-linked its currency from any standard, it simply printed notes to return those loans. People got a lot of cash in their hands and they started buying stuff. High demand fueled by a high quantity of currency and reduced levels of production (due to war) created a high mismatch between demand and supply. This caused "hyperinflation". This hyperinflation wiped out all the internal debt that had been accumulated by the German government during and after the war. The inflation was like a devastating earthquake that levelled the debt mountain.[2]

Whom Does Inflation Benefits?

The above explanation about Germany has a subtle point to be noted - the borrower (in this case the German government) benefited from inflation. Imagine that I borrowed $100 from a bank and made a chair from those $100. Due to inflation, the chair, instead of being sold at $150, has been sold at, say, $200. I still would be returning $110 to the bank (interest included). The loan that I have to return became a smaller piece of my income pie (which is $200 now instead of $150).

Now imagine the condition of a saver. Suppose I deposited $100 at the bank and have been told I would get $105 at the end of the year. When I get that $105 and go to buy something, my $105 would mean lesser than what it was a year back, because, in a world of 10% inflation, the thing that was costing $100 a year back now costs $110.

So, while putting money in bank deposits, keep in mind that the real return you are getting is (interest rate - inflation rate), and if you want to improve your financial condition, it is better to be an investor (either in equity or in asset) rather than a saver. Saving is meant for emergencies, not for prosperity. In most cases, currency-based savings erode the value of money.

3 "Inflation" - Not an Irrelevant Arcane Metric

Currency-based saving is meant only for emergencies. It should be in very liquid form (mainly bank deposits) and they shouldn't be more than a year of one's income. The rest of the money one has should go into well-studied investments in the form of physical or financial assets (say, shares or mutual funds). Also, consumption, which is the third avenue of usage of your money apart from saving and investment, should be watched closely!

Inflation significantly impacts salaried professionals. Their wages tend to be relatively sticky. In an inflationary environment, entrepreneurs and businesspersons usually insulate themselves by increasing the prices of their goods but the salaried people usually don't have this opportunity. Not many wage earners in an informal economy have their salaries indexed to inflation.

Let us now look into the types of inflation. Most of the time, inflation is measured in the form of Consumer Price Index (CPI), Wholesale Price Index (WPI) and Asset Price Index (API). The terms are rather self-explanatory, and if you are in business, keep an eye on WPI, and as an individual, keep an eye on CPI. The excessive borrowing by the government or structural decisions by it that shackles/hinders production almost always pushes up the inflation - remember that, for sure, it affects you!!

4

Basics of Business of Banking

The reach and maturity of the banking industry plays a vital role in the development and sustenance of an economy. Understanding the banking system is an important step in understanding the economy and its nuances. This chapter is an attempt at that step.

How did the banks come into existence? Why do they play such an important role in modern economic activities? How can banks avoid bad loans? To answer these questions, let us start with a simple scenario.

Imagine that I am a small trader living far away in an era when civilization just started. I visit a city for a pilgrimage and realize that there are no apple shops in this city. I feel that I can make good money if I start an apple trading company but I don't have money to buy land, a shed and the horse cart that are essential to sell apples. I go to a rich friend of mine who has hoards of money lying idle with him. I borrow 500 gold coins from my friend to cater to those needs and promise him that, for five years, from next year on, I will return him 108 gold coins for every 100 gold coins he gave me. This is called a long-term loan in current parlance.

Earning around 120 gold coins with my apple trade in the first year, I now have 12 gold coins at the end of the year (I gave 108 gold coins to my friend). Next year though, I don't need to buy land, shed or horse cart but I need around 30 gold coins to buy apples from the farm. I again go to my rich friend. He says he doesn't have readily available money, but given the fact that he is rich and famous, he gives a letter saying he guarantees to pay 30 coins on my behalf if I fail to pay. I take this letter and go to the farmer and get apples worth 30 gold coins. This is called "Letter of Undertaking" in modern finance terms. If my friend gives me 30 gold coins instead of the letter, it is called a working capital loan (the loan meant to run day-to-day affairs and not the long-term loan to buy land and shed).

Imagine that these transactions grew so big that one single rich guy couldn't afford to help me in trade. I go to a group of people who have pooled in their money and are lending to traders based on how good the traders are at doing business. This pool of money is called the bank.

This system goes well until all goes well but issues arise if something unforeseen happens. Suppose my horse cart overturns while going from farm to market or, say, the people in the new city in which I started trade don't develop a taste for apples and they simply don't buy my apples. Thus, I have spent 500 gold coins to buy land, shed and cart but no one is buying apples from me. I wouldn't be able to payback to my rich friend or to the group of people who have given me the loan. Basically, I turned into a "non-performing asset" for them.

Fast forward this system to the 21st century and it is still intact in more or less the same shape. We all pool in our excess money together at a place and call it the bank. And traders go to those banks and ask for money to run their affairs. Let's go into some detail.

Loan against Assets: If the person from whom I am taking the loan doesn't trust me of returning the money, I get my working capital loan (those 30 coins) by offering my land, shed or cart as a guarantee.

If a piece of land is offered as a guarantee or five horse carts that are equal in worth to that piece of land are offered as a guarantee, the banks will give more loan against land but may give lesser loan against the carts though the two assets are worth same. Because, in case of bankruptcy, it is easier to sell off land compared to selling off other assets (specialized machinery). Thus, land is a better quality mortgage than horse cart. Remember this point and I will come back to it while discussing other points.

What Happens In the Face of a Bad Loan

So what is the course of action when my cart overturns or I am not able to pay back a loan because no one is buying my apples? If I have been given a loan against the assets, as explained in the previous paragraph, my lenders would sell those assets and get back their money.

But they probably will not be able to get back the whole of their money. All people in the new city know that I am/my lenders are selling my land in distress and are in dire need to make the sale. They will buy my assets for just 400 gold coins instead of the actual worth of 500. The lenders agree to it taking only 400 coins. This, in modern parlance, is called "haircut".

The other scenario can be that I go to lenders and tell them that I will do some good promotion of my apples and am sure that next year I will be able to make big sale but for that, I need one more wallet of 20 gold coins. At times, trusting my trading instincts or due to the fact that there is a chance of getting all the money back rather than the 'haircut', the lenders do give another bag of 20 coins. Now you understand why banks give further loan to companies that didn't pay back the previous loans – It is due to the fact that they have a small hope that the light they see at the end of the tunnel is actual and not a mirage and thus the apple cart needs some more dose of coins!!!

Ways of checking creditworthiness:

By now you might have got convinced that the business of lending money in itself is a risky business. Banks need a decent understanding of the business to which they are giving a loan. To fulfill this need, lenders adopt two ways.

The first way is that there are clear rules and standards in the tribe about recording the affairs of the business. All the sales numbers are clearly and accurately noted down and are displayed in the Main Square of the village and lenders can clearly see that the business to which they are extending the loan is surely going to make money or is surely not going to make money. Knowing the creditor personally is not so important due to well-defined and proper rules. Modern-day financial reporting, auditing and book maintenance are part of this exercise.

The second way is a personal connection. Lenders give loans to people whom they know as men of honor and about whom they know that they have returned the loan every time in the last ten years. They know that they are men of intellect and have good expertise in the business and have been making sales every time they took up a business. Also, the lender personally knows the father of the man (those days, invariably, it used to be a man) whom he is giving money and the father will repay if the business of his son fails. In short, it is the social context and personal reasons that drive the decision to give a loan.

These two methods have been explained by Raghuram Rajan in his book 'Fault Lines'. He pointed that, to generalize, the Anglo-American firms, the ones from Australia, Canada, New Zealand, the United Kingdom and the United States usually operate at arm's length with their suppliers, lenders, customers and employees. They attribute both blame and rewards across the chain as they transact. In contrast, firms in continental Europe or Japan, rely on long-term relationships with suppliers, banks, customers and employees. They are more willing to share benefits and challenges with their associates. Their interactions are based more on long-term relationships rather than legal contracts.[1]

It has to be remembered that personal knowledge of debtors is a reasonable arrangement when the disclosure laws are not well developed and when it is just about trading apples in one city. But when it is about trading in multiple countries and with millions of dollars, such arrangements, sometimes, result in good money going behind bad money.

The reality is always in between these two extremes. Out of the above two mentioned methods, usually, countries that don't have a fully developed banking system deploy the latter. Here, the method of checking the creditworthiness of a person is based more on personal contact and less on numbers. The decision of whether to give a loan is dependent more on the rapport the debtor has with a bank than on the strength of his/her business. The loan disbursement decisions are taken on Friday nights rather than on Monday mornings and, eventually, the communities that historically have been doing business tend to get loans far more easily compared to those who are not historically traders. The rich and famous of the society tend to get loans far more easily compared to the good businessmen who are not rich and famous.

Now recall the point of land being a better quality mortgage than other assets. Because of this fact, the people and communities who historically have been custodians and owners of land tend to get loans easily vis a vis compared to people who don't have land, to begin with. In business, goodness is appreciated but power is rewarded. The distribution of wealth has elements of politics and it is not just about economic mechanisms.

How does it relate to common people

You might not have realized it but you are the rich friend of the trader and it is in your interest that the right methods are in place at banks to determine the creditworthiness of the trader since it is your money at risk.

To begin with, start understanding the affairs of corporate governance and finance. Take interest in ensuring that government puts the right disclosure rules and capital availability rules for banks and companies so that finances remain reasonably visible and stable. Also, governments should ensure that activist shareholders are strong enough and are protected enough by law. This will push the businessmen to avoid financial jugglery.

Laws that ensure that businesses have clearer corporate governance structures and their affairs are there in the public domain in much better and more detailed ways can go a long way to create economic prosperity – as they say, sunlight is the best disinfectant.

The government needs to have the right rules to keep in check the cartels. Lobbying by incumbents shouldn't be a disadvantage for newcomers in any industry. Competition brings forth efficiency. Land reforms might not seem to be relevant to bad loans, but it actually is one of the most important factors that can eliminate wealth distortion and ensure that money reaches those who are most efficient rather than those who are most privileged.

The above points are pretty boring, to put it mildly. Never can 'structural reforms' generate as much interest as, say, a high-profile arrest. Watching a 'right to information' bill being passed in parliament is far more boring compared to watching a big businessman being pushed into the police jeep and simply due to this reason that we the common people and, thus, the media enjoy watching individuals fall rather than focusing on reforming institutions.

Believing that one decisive individual ruler can correct our banking system and we need not wait to create reforms is like saying who will wait for years together to build a ship, I will swim across the ocean and reach the other shore!! A decisive individual ruler is good when we have a small pond to swim across but if it is about crossing an ocean we need a ship aka stronger institutions and vigilant travelers who should stay alert that the ship doesn't have any holes!! The banking industry relates to all of us. NPAs impacting it impacts all.

Social and Economic Impact of Banks

The spread of the banking system in a country is an important indicator of its economic maturity. Why is it so? Why is a financial industry a prerequisite for robust economic growth? Let us try to understand through a simple example.

4 Basics of Business of Banking

For the sake of simplicity, imagine that there are three banks in an economy, A, B and C, and there are three persons X, Y and Z. Suppose person X has an excess of $100 with him/her. S/he deposits it at bank A expecting the safety of money as well as hope that the bank will provide some return on the money. Bank A, after taking the deposit, doesn't hold the money in its lockers. Un-deployed money, whether stored under a mattress or in a bank safe, would be an unused opportunity. Now, the bank disburses it to, say, person Y. But the bank cannot disburse the complete $100 to person Y, since person X might withdraw some amount for his/her needs every now and then. Thus, a portion of the money, say, 80%, is lent out and the remaining amount is held at the bank to manage the withdrawal needs of its depositors.

Thus, person Y gets $80 from bank A. Now, suppose s/he deposits all the money in bank B. The cycle repeats for the third bank with which (as shown in the figure) $64 is remaining.

How this setup benefits the economy?

The excess money with person X that probably would have remained unused under his/her mattress is now being legally accessed by person Y who can use it for, say, starting a business. Thus, banks serve the primary purpose of facilitating human endeavors by arbitraging money between individuals. Credit catalyzes activity. It is an economic avatar of trust. Banks are distributors of this trust. Safe transfer of money between individuals is the prime purpose of banks and everything else, like safety, convenience, etc., is their secondary benefit.

Banks facilitate this movement of money and, as a by-product, create better liquidity in an economy through a phenomenon called the 'money multiplier effect'.

Part – I: Macroeconomics

The money multiplier effect can be understood through the following diagram. It can be seen in the diagram, that the actual money in the system is $100(of person X). But the money floating around because of banks lending is $144 (80+64).

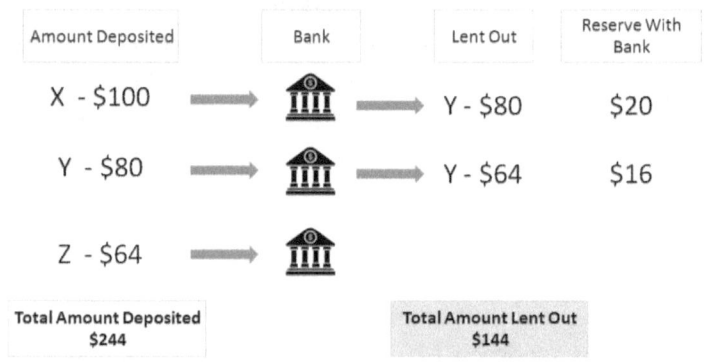

So, through banks, there is more money floating around in a system than the actual money that an economy has. Turn the idea the other way round and the logic still holds. If a person withdraws a dollar from the bank and keeps it under the mattress, the impact of that withdrawal is more than one dollar on the money that is circulating in the system.

The banking system depends on the simple assumption that everyone will not withdraw their complete money simultaneously. So, if a bank has 100 depositors and each has deposited $1000 into the bank, it would retain $20,000 (assuming 20% ratio) and lend across the remaining $80,000. It is a reasonable assumption that at any given point in time, $20,000 will be sufficient for the withdrawal needs of the 100 depositors. And this assumption survives as long as depositors trust that the bank would effectively handle the money and retrieve it from its borrowers at expected rates and in full. If for some reason, depositors lose this trust, all of them would rush simultaneously to banks to withdraw their money and the whole system might collapse (something on these lines happened during the 1929 depression). Indeed, the whole banking industry is an economic avatar of trust.

What are the pros and cons of a well-functioning and deeply penetrated banking system??

Pros:

- It generates borrowing opportunities for people.

Cons:

- It generates borrowing opportunities for people.

Yeah!!! Borrowing can be a double-edged sword. If individuals and businesses use the borrowed money for growing their business and generating value, they end up growing the economy with the same money that might have had been underutilized.

But if individuals and businesses use the same money for consumption beyond their repayment capacity, they end up bankrupt or, in the case of an underbelly financial transaction, a victim of a vicious circle of loans and extortion. The gist of the current chapter is that a well functioning, well spread, matured and just banking system is a prerequisite of a prosperous economy and is in the interest of everyone in the society.

5

Return on Capital vs. Return on Labor - How is It Related to Your Personal Wealth

The ethos instilled in us right from childhood make us believe that we can climb our way to wealth by sheer hardwork and putting in more and more hours at the office.

But basic economics says that getting rich is more to do with putting a larger portion of your money in investments rather than spending a larger portion of your time at the office. This chapter is an attempt to explain this idea in simple terms.

Imagine a city at beginning of time, where trading just started. Probably the city had 5 acres of arable land and a population of 10,000. Some 5 generations later, the population has increased to, say, 15,000, but the land still remains around 5 acres. So, the supply of labor has increased and thus its value reduced, but the supply of capital remained more or less the same, with more demand. Thus, the return on capital will naturally and significantly increase with every generation.

This phenomenon would have made the return on capital exponentially higher than the return on labor with passing time, but because of innovations of better means of production (online transactions don't need a 1500 square feet (sq ft.) physical bank), the need of capital has reduced but, still, it is more important than labor, which is abundantly available, thanks to population growth.

5 Return on Capital vs. Return on Labor...

Capital has a few other inherent advantages, and thus it provides better yield compared to labor.

- **Capital is more inheritable:** It passes down from parents to children much more easily compared to labor. A carpenter attempting to teach nuances of carpentry to his son might not be sure that the kid might get 100% of what he is teaching, but a landlord, giving 5 hectares of land to his daughter can be 100% sure that the girl has 5 hectares of land. This aspect ensures a head start for the next generation of those who are contributing capital to the production compared to the next generation of those who are contributing labor to the production.
- **Capital is more cross deployable:** Shares of, say,$1000 of a toy factory can be sold and replaced with shares worth $1000 of an e-commerce firm. Similarly, a factory that was being used for making toys, with some effort, can be turned into a warehouse of an e-commerce firm. Whereas, a person who was an expert at handling toy-making machines might find it extremely difficult to find a job in an e-commerce warehouse that provides him/her as much as s/he used to earn at toy factory. The persons can indeed re-skill themselves and capital can go obsolete (toy-making machines can't be deployed in an e-commerce firm), but relatively speaking, the ease of cross deployment of capital is far better compared to cross deployment of labor.
- **Capital is easily divided into chunks:** If a capitalist has $1000, s/he can deploy $500 each in, say, a technology giant and an auto-manufacturing firm. If one of the two industries gets impacted, at least the other one can provide

ease to the capitalist. Whereas, the person providing his/her labor would find it extremely difficult to provide services in two companies. Even in the rare case in which a person is working two jobs, s/he would most likely work in very similar industries. The two companies in which the person would be working would usually be co-related and might go bust simultaneously if something adverse happens. Risk mitigation by spreading your portfolio is relatively easy in the capital than in labor.

- **Capital doesn't lose its abilities along with the abilities of the person deploying it:** If you are an engineer who earns by calculating adroitly, you may lose your abilities with age and thus after a certain age, the returns that your labor is providing you (income) will not be same as it used to be when you were at your prime. The same doesn't happen with capital. If you own a certain number of shares, the returns they are providing are not dependent on your health. Thus, capital is something that can help you when you are in dire need, unlike labor that evaporates with your health.

- **Capital stands a better chance of security against job losses due to automation:** The emerging trend of automation and companies generating high revenues with few employees might render quite a few people jobless in the future. If the person who has gone jobless due to automation has some capital invested in the companies of the new economy, then there are chances that s/he would be part owner of the robots that took his/her job. This, in turn, would create an economic safety net that would be much stronger than an economic safety net created through re-skilling or minimum wages.

5 Return on Capital vs. Return on Labor...

So, if you want to improve your living standards, get your finger in the capital pie.... bit by bit, piece by piece, as much your income allows you so that slowly but surely, you climb the social mobility ladder.

Financial innovations of current times have created an easy way to do this: Company stocks

If you can't afford to buy a factory, better buy a "share" of that factory. Instead of considering the stock exchange a casino, consider it an opportunity to buy a square foot of the factory of the firm whose shares are being traded. Analyze the business on grounds of common sense and basic financials and revenues. Invest and then hold for a few decades. As the business grows, you receive its returns.

But share trading can affect you adversely if done wrong. If you purchase a stock that is overpriced compared to its actual revenues, it will catch up with you eventually. For example, after the rise of stock prices in 1901, there was a 20-year decline and stocks didn't rise till the bull market of 1920. Also, while the Great Depression of 1929 lasted only until WWII, the S&Ps Composite Index didn't return to its 1929 value until 1958.[1]

Ensure the following points while investing.

1. Shares that you are buying have steady income across years (no spikes/big falls) and actually make a profit (During the 1999 stock bubble, some companies were actually in loss but their shares were touching skies just because they had. com at the end of their names).
2. Have a business model that might not get easily affected by technology disruptions. Warren Buffet calls it a moat.

3. Choose a company that has a P/E ratio lower than its industry peers – it is just a heuristic rule.
4. Ben Graham used to say that one should invest in a company and not in an industry.
5. Invest in a chunk of companies, so that fluctuations of a single company don't wipe off your wealth.
6. Take it slow. Anyone promising quick riches is either duping you or is a fool himself and mostly it is both.

Is the idea of better ROI on capital relevant even in the future?

Now coming back to the point of capital giving a better ROI, a question that usually comes to one's mind is: Do we still need capital? We usually feel that the industrial revolution has reduced its need and now the digital revolution has completely eliminated its need. You no longer need a 1500 sq ft. bank and, moving forward, you probably won't even need a 10000 sq ft. shopping mall. Two things counter this argument:

- Though the entertainment, financial transactions, a part of education and a good deal of information management has gone completely digital, but our need for food, shelter, clothing, transport and physical entertainment is not going anywhere anytime soon. We still would need land and machines to achieve these things, that too for a population that would probably peak at 1.5 times the current levels.
- The automation and mechanization that would be needed in coming times would need far bigger and far more complex capital investment. We are moving into an era in which the problems that we are solving

are becoming increasingly mammoth and complex. Discovering a new atomic particle is no longer about passing light through a small slit. You would need far more accurate and sophisticated machines that are produced, maintained and used by thousands of people. Planning private rocket launches and creating public transport would need far bigger physical assets. All this would need capital. Probably more of it, rather than less of it. Thus, the idea of return on capital is more than return on labor is going to stick around in foreseeable future.

The relative number of "super craftsmen" - those who buy their private islands through their programming skills or being famous doctors is for sure on the rise but the proportion of people living off accumulated, invested and inherited wealth is still far more common. So, for those with no such extraordinary programming skills, moving a chunk of our savings into capital investments is as, or rather more, important than our next promotion at the office.

An anecdote associated with Rockfeller, would be a befitting end to this chapter. It is said that he used to lend small amounts of money to others when he himself was a young poverty-stricken boy. He related that he used to save little sums of money and learned that he could get as much interest for $50 loaned as he could earn by digging potatoes for ten days.[2]

6

Exports vs. Imports: A Tussle Involving Economics as Well as Politics

Deliberations around national prosperity inevitably involve imports and exports. It is usually considered part of economic prudence that a country should double down on exports and cut down its imports. And to meet this end, subsidized exports and high tariffs on imports are considered good policies. And most of the measures around these tariffs are political live wires and any discussion around such measures avalanche into heated debates.

This chapter is about dissecting the import vs. export debate and an attempt to understand the pros and cons of different measures that are taken to regulate trade between countries.

Adam Smith, the brilliant economist pointed out that one doesn't attempt to make at home what costs him more to make than to buy. A tailor does not attempt to make his own shoes but buys them from a shoemaker. The shoemaker does not attempt to make his own clothes but employs a tailor. The same idea can be extended to complete countries.[6] If a foreign country can supply us for a cost that is cheaper compared to ours, better buy it from them, while we supply to them the product that we are better at production.

So, the idea of import is like purchasing something rather than producing it in-house. If you are a programmer, you are better off if you write programs and deploy a teacher to teach your kids. Though you probably know how to teach math to a fourth-grader, still you consider it prudent to employ a teacher because that will leave you with the time that you can profitably deploy to earn more than what you are paying to the teacher. If the watch-maker of another country is good at producing wrist-watches at 100 units of your currency and your country's watch-maker is producing the same at 120 units, then you, as a consumer, are better off by 20 units if you get the foreign-made wrist-watch rather than the one made inside the country. You can use those spare 20 units for consumption or investment and, as a whole, this would benefit your country. Probably, your country is a better textile producer and thus it makes economic sense for natives (and thus the government) of another country to buy textiles from your country. It would leave them with a few spare units of money. The logic behind promoting barrier-less trade between countries is as simple as this.

Then why are exports considered good and imports bad in most of the discussions around imports vs. exports?

Below are a few reasons:

1. Probably the prime reason is the way all of us are organized. You might easily come across "watch-makers association" but have you ever come across "watch-buyers association"? When the decision of allowing the import of 100 units worth of watches is taken, the watch-producers who are few and relatively organized easily represent their concerns to the government pointing out that their

revenue is down due to cheap imports and their companies and their employees are facing adverse impact due to this decision. They will also request support for exports pointing out that exports will provide them revenue from a new market and thus bring new tax sources for the government. But the consumers who are a lot many and seldom organized into a group barely notice that they are paying 20 units more on each wrist-watch they are buying if imports are banned. Rarely does someone argue on behalf of those 'forgotten many'.

2. I don't have research to back up this idea, but probably the second reason is historic. Historically, trade between people as well as between two countries used to almost always happen in gold. Buying something from a foreign country used to make a country lose its gold. This used to lead to a reduction in the number of gold coins within the boundary of a country. Fewer coins but the same amount of grains/cotton/sheep etc. in a country meant that the same amount of goods is being chased by lesser currency. Suppose a shepherd wanted to sell his sheep but the people of the city had fewer gold coins, then the shepherd would agree to sell his sheep for fewer gold coins since that is better than letting the sheep die. This phenomenon is called deflation –the falling of prices (here, in terms of the number of gold coins). Deflation has two adverse effects – a. purchasers stop buying, hoping that prices will fall further, and b. producers stop producing, since they are getting lesser profits with every passing day. Deflation can bring the whole economy to a standstill (You can read the chapter on currency to understand the dynamics between goods and currency). This probably was the reason why imports

were considered bad for the economy of a country. But today, rarely, a country pegs its currency to gold. Most of the international trade is conducted in dollars or mutually agreed upon currencies. The quantity of currency in circulation is based on economic activity rather than a particular metal. But the memory of a particular metal, straitjacketing the economy is still with us and thus probably there is a general aversion to imports.

- **Subsidized exports:** Since the common perception is that exports are beneficial, many governments subsidize them. But if we dig a bit deeper, we can understand the flaw in subsidized exports. Suppose the country that is supplying wrist-watches at 100 units/piece, is not actually good at producing cheaper watches, rather its government is supporting the watch-makers. It means that the government is taxing its people and giving that money to producers and thus in turn to the foreign citizens!! It would be ill-informed happiness on part of the populace if they feel happy about the government giving away their hard-earned money to people of another country.

If things are so simple and self-evident, then why there are barriers to trade and why do countries shut themselves out rather than trading more? Let us add a few practicalities to the debate of import vs. export to understand what can be the exceptional situations when appropriate regulations can be considered as an alternative to free trade.

Products & Technologies of National Importance: Nations should ensure that they are preserving the production know-how and industrial ecosystems of the products and services that are important for their sovereignty - products relevant to defense, food and essential healthcare are primary candidates in this list. Trading with other countries for these categories shouldn't completely be based on cost considerations. Rather, minimal know-how should be maintained in-house so that in face of hostility, the other country should not be able to arm-twist the nation by stopping the supply of essential products like food or medicines.

Nurturing an Industry in its Infancy: If a country is attempting the creation of an industry from scratch, it makes sense for it that the industry is supported through tax exemptions, subsidies and training ecosystem. Import of similar products isinitially discouraged so that the industry picks up its ropes as it treads on the learning curve. But it should be noted this is a rather sticky "exception"... it has a habit of sticking around... almost every export subsidy and import tariff is imposed citing this need of defending the growing local industry. Usually, industries get habituated to these favors that are given to them in the initial stages and even after maturing fully, they act like a grownup who is still dependent on his/her parents for basic needs. These supports should be time-bound and should be erected along with a clear date of dismantling - which is practically a very difficult thing to achieve.

Lack of Level Playing Field: In some cases, the difference in cost of production between countries occurs because one of the countries involved is not giving consideration to, say, environmental laws or has relaxed labor protection requirements for their firms. Suppose one country requires its watch-makers that the by-products of manufacturing are properly treated before being released outside, whereas the other country simply allows its manufacturers to dump the by-products on open land… the difference in prices is not on account of adroit manufacturers, it is simply due to the non-level playing field between the two countries. In such a scenario, countries should ensure that through different political and economic means, the playing field is made level rather than shutting out the trade.

To conclude, it must be noted that the above-mentioned exceptions shouldn't become the norm in deciding the trade between countries. Trade between countries can bring prosperity to them the way trade between two individuals specialized in their field brings them prosperity and saves them the drudgery of performing every task on their own.

7

Impact of State and Mega Firms on Individual Prosperity

Anyone attempting a hop to the next economic station of life has to tackle many things. A lot of external factors influence the kind of opportunities available to the individual. Two institutions, state and corporate organizations, given their size, are very important among these external factors.

Influence of State on Economic Prosperity and Money Distribution

An extreme example of how an individual's chance at prosperity can be influenced by state regulations can be understood by citing the situation of a slave in earlier days. Slaves had to toil in the most hazardous and arduous conditions and the existing ideology deprived them of even basic rights – a detestable situation completely sanctioned by the state. Eventually, slavery became something unacceptable on account of the development of human ideology, still, there is a paradox when slavery was abolished in the 1800s - all the discussions around abolition used to be focused on how the masters of those slaves should be compensated when the slaves are freed. It was the slaves who were exploited, but the focus of compensation post emancipation was on

7 Impact of State and Mega Firms on Individual Prosperity

masters since they lost 'property'. The political, regulatory and ideological wisdom of the time was a mega factor in the slave's shot at prosperity or rather a lack of it even after emancipation. And the aspects of ideology and regulatory statutes still play a big role in the economic progress of different sections of society. Politics and economics are inseparable. The distribution of money has been eternally dependent upon the underlying ideas that justify awarding (property, patents, licenses, etc.) or demanding (taxes, tributes, etc.) of means of production.

The remarkable development of humanity in the last two or so centuries is owed to the fact that the emerging ideologies across the world subscribed to the idea that prosperity is not a vice. The societies where rule of law and meritocracy are relatively nearer to ideal have a more equitable distribution of wealth. They provide better survival tools to the weakest person and thus more prosperous society. The societies that justified rules and methods that protected ownership rights of one section of society and curbed freedom of another (say, that of slaves) on account of race or caste or religion ended up with stunted economies that had marble graves for one section and starving days for another.

Improved ideologies and governance systems are as important an invention as the steam engine when it comes to the creation of modern society. The contemporary world owes its existence to ideas of uniform opportunity, rule of law, transactional liberty, rule-driven rather than individual-driven institutions as much as it does to material inventions.

If anything, the influence of rules on individual prosperity has increased due to bigger roles being played by governments in our lives. In the good old days, the affairs handled by the government were rather limited and simple. The resource distribution problems solved by governments of medieval times were as simple as the demarcation of common grazing lands and usage of water bodies. These problems have now given way to complex and far more seminal issues. For example, the right utilization of public money for fundamental research, management of telecom spectrum for communication, allocation of mining rights, designing educational policies, etc. need specialized understanding. Whether to use available money to create a new research institute or a hospital for the poor? These complex problems deserve far more public scrutiny and public awareness.

A disinterested citizenry is one of the major threats to modern society, democracy and mass prosperity. Uninterested people would mean that any inherent distortion in the distribution of resources and thus wealth will magnify over a few generations to shift the power and prosperity to the advantaged class. Awareness of the trend of policies is far more important for individuals in the management of current forms of wealth. Ignorance might be bliss, but this bliss is better avoided if you want to improve your economic conditions.

Almost all matters of politics influence economic access, but speed and structure of justice delivery, taxation, universal access to fundamental education, corporate regulation and monetary policies take lion's share of the pie of this influence. Also, a basic guardrail to deciding the role of the state is that only the collective problems that are difficult for masses or organizations to solve at an individual level (say, a dam or a highway) should involve government. State, if present in any sector that could have been better handled by the market, only acts as a hurdle. Economist Milton Friedman used to joke that if government bureaucrats should ever gain control of the Sahara, there soon would be a shortage of sand.[1]

7 Impact of State and Mega Firms on Individual Prosperity

The second most important aspect of a civilized welfare state is that government should take collective care of the section of society that is weak due to its circumstances since such care is an indicator of an imitable society. Governments would need to have possible safety nets so that no person who lost employment on account of physical disability or economic irrelevance should be reduced to starving, or no child should lose a shot at basic education and thus opportunity on account of his/her low parental income or no poor should get a debilitating economic blow due to health emergency.

The citizenry would be required to understand their stakes when decisions are being taken around the policies that decide the distribution of common resources in terms of, say, implementation of patent regimes, usage of fundamental research by commercial organizations and access to information and access to education. People usually vote by foot, by emigrating over a period of time, when these complex maneuvers are ill-managed by a certain government.

But both the powers that be as well as the citizenry should understand that things have to be better than just voting by foot. Societies with ill-developed and partial laws, influence-driven execution and social maneuvering-driven resource management are only a shackle on efficient use of global resources. Understanding and upholding laws, figuring out their right mix (say, for example, in the case of patents – how many years of exclusive access to the patent is too many years?) is a messy affair and would need sustained education and patient experimental learning on part of both governments and people, but it is for sure worth it. The governments that tend to be content with existing power structures and rely on under-informed masses for their survival are only undermining the growth potential of their own countries. The same applies for individuals and it is in their own interest that people should understand how policies are being managed and having a free and fair government might not be apparent but is a sure way of achieving long-term economic prosperity for the masses. Otherwise, an inefficient government, with its monopoly on legal violence, will collect taxes from people or usurp common resources, without providing commensurate services.

Having touched upon the importance of the state in economic prosperity, let us pivot to the market. The state, despite its omnipresence, cannot solve all the problems of economics. When it comes to economics, it has to be strategized by the state but should be executed by the market.

Influence of Corporate Organizations on Economic Prosperity

Contrasting corporate with countries should begin with a quote from the brilliant novel 'Shantaram' by Gregory David Roberts. He points out that the force more ruthless and cynical than the business of big politics is the politics of big business.

Given the extraordinary size and global presence of commercial firms, they have become more conspicuous in the lives of individuals and they have started wielding significant power. The fact that there are some global organizations, whose revenue is higher than the GDPs of some countries and who have (almost) uniform policies across the globe when contrasted with the reality of the absence of a global regime to tame, manage and negotiate these organizations should make us ponder about the distortions such huge power, answerable only to profit motives, can have on employment, money distribution, and environment.

7 Impact of State and Mega Firms on Individual Prosperity

Commercial organizations have started to play a much bigger part in our social identities lately. For example, persons working for certain mega-firms have access to, say, stupendous health insurance and extraordinary gratuity privileges, which, say, a self-employed person or a person working in the informal sector can only dream of. Probably, in current times, being employed by certain firms has started to play the same role as being from a certain caste or class or tribe played in the olden days.

Individuals seldom have the power to, say, get into a legal arbitration with organizations who have wronged them as either employers or suppliers. The means of managing legal litigations available to organizations is usually exponentially higher compared to those available to individuals.

These mega difference between the interacting entities – individuals vs. firms – essentially calls that the third entity, that is, the state, should ensure regulations that make the playing field more level. This might mean having rules in terms of, say, minimum monetary benefits to individuals in case of termination of services or, say, implementation of equitable terms of service that prevent exploitation of information asymmetry in the market or, say, providing the right of collective bargaining to employees, etc.

Also, the incumbent organizations not only have an asymmetric relationship with their employees and customers but also with new entrants in their industry. They use levers like patents to hinder innovation or use their deep pockets to acquire new entrants. Economist Alferd Kahn remarked that the great research laboratories are incidentally technological centers. They manufacture patents from the point of view of the business.[2]

It is very rational on part of organizations, to try and block new entrants in an industry so that they can have healthy profits, but it is equally rational on part of government and individuals to keep an eye on such behavior and limit it so that it doesn't harm the collective prosperity. Appropriate monopoly laws and patent management are important tools in this regard. The detailed analysis of these laws is beyond the capability of this writer, but nevertheless is an important economic tool.

Having the right balance of regulations is extremely important. The rules should neither scuttle the firms at one extreme nor should leave the individuals to a ruthless jungle competition in the name of a free market. Understanding the complex maneuvering of underlying rules and their right implementation for running organizations is extremely important for individual prosperity.

8

Opportunities and Trends in the Next Wave of Progress

In his book 'Capitalism in America', Alan Greenspan points out the contribution of 'electric servants' to American life. The electric iron, vacuum cleaners, washing machines, refrigerators and electric sewing machines that proliferated during the 1920s ensured that people got spare time to further participate in economic activity and spurred the era of mass abundance and consumption. These electric servants replicated this pattern of mass prosperity proliferation in whichever country they touched so much so that an average person in the 21st century has access to luxuries of extreme speeds, temperature control and food served from far away geographies. These luxuries weren't accessible even to the richest person in the world just a century back.

But these electric servants and their grandchildren (computers and artificial intelligence) have their side effects that are manifesting in the form of pollution, climate change, overcrowding, income inequality and rendering of a class of people economically irrelevant. So, the next wave of progress would not just grapple with economic questions rather the thought leaders and organizations would be required to answer the questions and parameters around equitable value distribution, climate change and crowding of cities, and other similar problems arising due to abundance rather than shortage. Profit still captures the lion's share of companies' imagination pie, but there are chances that the societies and companies which consider a few more parameters like social impact, and pollution might save the day, save themselves and lead the next wave of progress.

This might sound like overstretched imagination but one can contrast this idea with medieval kingdoms of Asia and Europe. They were more or less at the same level of prosperity, but one set of kingdoms put their money behind poetry, philosophy, theology and elaborate rituals, whereas the other set, probably out of serendipity, tilted towards the nascent, rather almost non-existent fields of science and finance. We, with a 20-20 hindsight, can't help but feel surprised at how naïve the former set might have been not to have bothered about science and technology and ended up way behind in terms of prosperity and collective wealth. High are the chances, that a few centuries from now, the generations might find us naïve that we were focused on money, GDP and per capita energy produced, etc., whereas it should have been climate impact parameters, social impact indices, human development indices and common good that should have had been at the center stage of our decision-making forums.

Thus the development of the coming century, irrespective of the field would require deeper understanding of their broader effect on societies. For example, as of this writing in 2021, some countries have already allowed the incorporation of for-profit companies, which have a positive impact on society, workers and the environment in addition to profit as their legally defined goals. Such organizations are called 'benefit corporations' in legal parlance. Similarly, the Human

Development Index initiated by Amartya Sen, which considers three aspects of access to health, education, and goods is a serious attempt to replace GNP as a sole indicator of economic prosperity.[1], [2] Yet another example is the doughnut economics that has been proposed by Kate Raworth. She presented economics as a doughnut whose outer ring is the ecological ceiling that shouldn't be crossed and the inner ring is the social foundation that should be sustained. She proposed that economic activity should be carried out in between these two rings and has identified various factors to ensure this compliance.[3]

Post this preamble, this chapter probes three industries that touch our everyday life, have improvement room, might need some amelioration and with some conscious and collaborated effort probably can unlock benefits for many other aspects of our life – The industries picked up are transportation, healthcare and education. These industries don't take the lion's share of the pie in economic terms nor are they currently as happening as, say, data management or artificial intelligence but they are likely to have a significant impact on the broader set of metrics discussed in previous paragraphs. The discussion being presented here is more in terms of costs, operations and impact on the economy rather than technological specifics that are unraveling and propelling the change in these industries.

Commute

In business jargon, the commute is a need that can be catered to by a 'commodity' service – say, public transport, taxis etc. But throughout the last century, partially owing to inefficiencies of those commodity services and partly due to the desire of self-expression, the major part of this commodity has been catered to through individual branded cars. These cars served the purpose of indicating wealth and personal success and provided comfortable and independent means of commute. But they are relatively inefficient means of commute. To move around an individual weighing 60 kg, a vehicle weighing 1200 kg is deployed. Often, cars need two persons when one has to go to a destination (Your chauffeur doesn't have any business at your office, but s/he accompanies you there every day). To move around one person, a vehicle that occupies space of around 5 individuals is deployed on a road. Even a well-used car remains parked for almost 90% of its life. Slowly, these inefficiencies in terms of energy consumption, space and labor intensity (due to the need for a chauffeur) have started eating into the only USPs the individual vehicles provide, comfort and independence, by manifesting themselves in the form of chronic traffic jams, global warming, pollution and parking hassles.

Left to demand-supply, the problem of commute is not yet efficiently being solved and is up for better solutions. And addressing the problem of commute in terms of pollution reduction, crowding elimination and not just profits would need special attention from automobile suppliers, consumers and governments.

Lawrence D Burns, in his book 'Autonomy', dissected the trends around the future of commute and predicted that the future of achieving far better commute with far fewer resources is very much within reach. He considered self-driving cars at the forefront of this future. These cars would avoid the extra person on the wheel and thus would improve efficiency. Also, the cars will constantly move around, serving customers rather than remaining parked. He felt that in about 2007-08 itself, the technical pieces of the autonomous driving puzzle were very much in place and only regulatory or infra pieces were missing.[4] As of 2021, self-driving cars have become reality and the companies pioneering them have cumulatively driven them for millions of miles.[5]

Mass adoption of self-driving cars, apart from being a technological marvel, is going to have a significant impact on energy, space and human capital utilization. By virtue of being self-driven, they would improve things in terms of:

1. Physical space by avoiding the seat that is usually reserved for the chauffeur.
2. Labor costs by avoiding driver who charges money for his/her services.
3. Asset utilization by not being parked for too long.
4. Being fast and avoiding traffic congestion, since we would need smaller and lesser vehicles (since they are being utilized day and night).
5. Energy utilization by being smaller and programmed to run at optimal speeds.
6. Safer by avoiding the common errors that human drivers might commit.

Another significant trend in automobiles is the movement towards electrical propulsion compared to gasoline propulsion. The primary driver of this trend would probably be the low carbon footprint of electrical vehicles over their life cycle compared to gasoline vehicles. Electric vehicles tend to be environmentally friendly even if they are getting power from carbon-intensive grids.[6] They are also relatively better in terms of maintenance by virtue of their lesser number of moving parts.

If these trends are a panacea compared to current mobility solutions, why are they yet to become mainstream? The following are probably the primary reasons for the delay in the mass adoption of self-driving and electric-propelled cars:

- Large-scale changes would be required in manufacturing technology, operations and infrastructure. These changes need reorientation efforts in terms of research, marketing, operations, etc. on part of incumbent automobile companies. Overcoming the inertia inherent in incumbents, who face the 'innovators dilemma' famously posited by Clayton Christensen, requires either new players in the industry or independent satellite entities of existing players, either of which requires a lot of effort, capital and foresight.
- The creation of cross-disciplinary newer infrastructure, like IT-enabled traffic signals, e-vehicle charging points with reasonable frequency, newer forms of machine tools to manufacture electric engines, electronic vision assisted parking spots, etc., are usually constrained by the existing infrastructure which is still serving its useful life. For example, electric power displaced steam power in factories only when factories were rebuilt to use multiple small motors rather than one single large engine.[7] This pace of replacement of old with new is catalyzed by benefits of new but would, for sure, be slowed down by remaining utility still being supplied by old.
- The spread of technology and its commercialization is more dependent on the economic situation of its users and less on the intrinsic qualities of innovation. The majority of technology adopters don't ask "What can the technology do?", rather they ask "How much will

I benefit by using the technology?". Autonomous, low footprint commutes, too, would be needed to face the same questions and wouldn't be meted out with special treatment by consumers just for being technological miracles.

Its precise form and shape might still be amorphous, but for sure the future of commute is one comprising shared, low energy-consuming, low carbon-intensive and probably autonomous vehicles, complete with digitization that would help in vehicle sharing and personalized entertainment. The trends around autonomy, electrification and 'electronification' are blending in myriad ways for vehicles and would need a newer mix of infrastructure and skills. We would need programmers who are good at route planning, capacity analytics and system engineering. We probably would need traffic signals that have both light signals and QR codes. We would require individuals who can convert traffic rules into algorithms and would need lawyers, insurance inspectors and regulators who can understand the nuances of algorithms. The growth that is to ensue in this industry has a lot of opportunities for entrepreneurs, businesspersons and, of course, end users.

Healthcare and Pharmaceutical Industry

The second industry that might play a significant role in our future lives would probably be healthcare and pharmaceuticals. Universal healthcare access can be one of the major levers of equity and the spread of prosperity in future society.

The healthcare industry is unique in multiple ways, a few of which are listed here:

- **Role of influencers:** The prime source of healthcare diagnostics, drugs and treatment purchases are not the consumers, rather the influencers (doctors decide which medicine are you supposed to take, not you). This creates significant information asymmetry in the system between consumer and supplier, which, in turn, leads to a market that doesn't flex smoothly on principles of demand and supply.
- **Licensing:** The effect of a mistake in production or consumption can be devastating and, at times, fatal. Thus, the professional licensing requirements in the healthcare industry are significant and create a natural scarcity because permissions and licensing set the pace for many factors of healthcare supply.
- **Research:** The role of R & D and patents is far more pronounced in the pharmaceutical industry in terms of pricing, than, say, the fashion industry or, say, FMCG, though the consumption cycle is more or less as recurring as the above two.
- **Pricing:** The price of medicines is rather un-elastic, that is, the consumption is not much dependent on price. And also, on the other side, some governments levy price controls for medicines.
- **Compulsory licensing:** This is yet another controversial topic that is frequently discussed in the pharmaceutical industry. A few countries have the rule that if they deem a medicine essential for their public, they force the patent-holding company of that medicine to license production to other companies as well so that there are multiple players in the market.

Due to these attributes, the healthcare industry has taken a unique form and shape, which is enigmatic, has a dose of intellectualism, and is managed through heavy regulation. Also, this being an essential industry, public discussion around healthcare, usually, is high in terms of political and emotional decibels.

The scientific trends in the industry are towards biotech medicines, gene therapy leads to individualized medicines and digitization of diagnostics. But rather than focusing on these trends, the discussion in the ensuing paragraphs is focused on levers that can ensure smoother operations for healthcare. What can lead to cheaper, unclogged and efficient customer-centric operations, rather than healthcare provider-centric operations so as to ensure better access at lesser costs? Ensuring that the future developments in this industry enable cost-effective access to the poor would be an important prerequisite for mass access to prosperity.

Most of the products and services find their way to people if left to market forces, except in cases where the market fails to perform efficiently due to market failures. Two potential market failures in healthcare are scarcity and imperfect information.[8] Anybody who has searched for an expert surgeon for their parents and found one with difficulty but found him/her too costly to afford might be convinced of scarcity in healthcare and anyone who came to know about a treatment or a diagnostic test precisely while undergoing it need not be convinced about imperfect information. The incentive of maintaining scarcity in the pharmaceutical industry is so high that some firms undertake "killer" acquisitions, acquisitions are undertaken only to shutdown promising drug projects that can compete with firms' existing drugs.[9]

How can these hindrances to an efficient market be eliminated for the healthcare industry? The pointers in the next paragraphs trace the trends in the industry and probe which aspects of the industry can unlock efficiency.

Regulation:

Healthcare and pharmaceuticals is an industry in which regulatory intervention is essential as well as high. Identifying improvement opportunities in regulation can hopefully unlock a lot of the supply potential of the industry. The primary focus of regulations is manufacturing, pricing and patent enforcement. The manufacturing regulations cover aspects of record-keeping (physical and electronic), personnel training, facility management and related hygiene, and storage. The pricing restrictions in certain countries have manifested due to healthcare infrastructure shortages and the relative inelasticity of pharmaceutical prices. In many countries, governments maintain a list of essential medicines and allow companies to price those essential medicines on a cost plus fixed profit basis so as to ensure that the particular medicine is available at a lower price. This, at times, has an unintended effect of organizations staying away from certain countries hindering availability at the cost of affordability. The idea of compulsory licensing pointed out in previous paragraphs, too, is a classic tug of war between availability and affordability.

The right amount of regulation in this sector would be all about keeping it relevant to the "truth of time", keeping it iterative and stable rather than abrupt. It would keep the industry thriving as well as would keep it "healthy" enough to serve the general public.

The potential digital ideas and trends in regulation to help in the smooth functioning of the industry are:

- Data-driven decision-making: Use of algorithms and models for regulatory purposes. For example, the Food and Drug Administration (FDA), the drug authority of USA, has initiated a use case in which they are deploying artificial intelligence to identify potentially violative seafood products[10]
- Use of digital twin for real-time tracking of adherence to manufacturing regulations of cleanliness, right dosage and process control
- Blockchain technology deployment for tracing medicine distribution networks and their ownership
- Edge computing for managing and monitoring the storage condition of in-transit medicines

These are just a few pointers to bring home the point that technology deployment for the healthcare industry can open up multiple opportunities for tech entrepreneurs and can help in better functioning of the industry and eliminate a few of the market inefficiencies associated with it.

Operations:

Let us pivot our focus on the next question: Can access to pharmaceuticals be improved by taking a cue from the wave of growth in the computing and digital industry? The computing industry started as an esoteric field that was initially thought of only for geeks and mega-companies and research labs but it ended up providing far more digital power to the masses at a far less price compared to what was available even to the mightiest organizations at the beginning of the industry.

Such a swift growth marked by the fall in the cost of computing power has ensured an efficient mass production market. Can the future pharmaceutical industry be a cost-driven horizontal industry (HI) the way the computing industry has gone?

In his book "Only Paranoid Survive", Andrew Grove narrated how the computer industry turned into a horizontal industry. The computer industry was vertically-oriented (each company had its own "make to sell" chain) at the beginning of the '80s. It turned into a horizontally oriented industry (chips being made by one player, computers by another and software by yet another) within a decade.

Is the pharmaceutical industry up for a similar transition? Probably the product attributes of the pharmaceutical industry can throw some light on this question. How does a consumer chooses a product? A product is chosen initially for functionality. Then, once a consumer has multiple products with the same functionality, then the choice evolves to the product with better reliability, then to convenience and finally to price.[11] To elaborate: Suppose you want to choose between two laptops, you check their features and are ready to pay a premium on the first one if it has relevant (need not be better) features compared to the second one. If the two have the same features (functionality), then you check which one has lesser breakdowns and you choose that one. If you realize that both the models have fairly same maintenance needs (equally reliable), then it is about which one is lighter to handle and if the laptops are twins in this aspect, then you would prefer the cheaper option!!! This phenomenon is the same for almost all things being traded and medicines are no exception.

Suppose you went to buy paracetamol. Which brand would you choose? If you are sure that the available brands have the same functionality and reliability (which the regulator ensures), then it is about whether it is available at the shop near you (convenience) and then it is about which one is cheaper. Though the consumption dynamics in pharmaceuticals are slightly different due to the presence of influencers (doctors) and the presence of pharma benefit managers, they too give a lot of importance to cost-effective medicines. Thus, it would be a good thing if the future of pharma is more cost-effective by being horizontally integrated. Horizontal integration would mean basic chemicals would be made by one manufacturer, those basic chemicals would be converted into complex ingredient by another and those ingredients would be converted into pills by yet another firm.

The speed of move towards horizontal integration might be slower due to trust/brand recognition among influencers, but with increased vigilance of regulators and increased awareness among consumers, the industry will eventually have a customer base that would be indifferent to the brand and would be conscious of price. Regulators would probably play a pivotal role in building trust among consumers and this trend might pick up the pace.

There are couple of factors that would push the industry towards cost-driven horizontal integration. Primary would be economies of scale in basic chemical manufacturing (suppliers). It means that if produced in bulk and with bigger batches, chemicals tend to be cheaper. Basic chemical manufacturing is capital-intensive, thus it would tend to have fewer but bigger players. Pharmaceutical benefit managers (PBMs) (prominent in the US industry) also would be major infulencers in the push toward cost orientation. There might be a few factors that counter the move, say for example high switching cost from one raw material provider to another (due to regulatory requirements). But such factors might slow down the transformation, not eliminate it. If the government ensures better regulation so that even the unknown players abide by the requisite quality control, then the future would be that of cost-effective access to medicine and it can help a lot of people.

What should pharmaceutical companies do in face of this transformation?

What can a company do in the face of HI transformation? How can pharma manufacturing organizations that have prominently safeguarded their market share by focusing on patents survive in a future that would be more cost-focused? Here are a few ideas:

- Do not move upstream (that is, into basic chemical manufacturing) through capital investment. Rather, have long-term pacts with multiple vendors, complete with penalties when they are not able to supply as per agreed timelines and quality to ensure risk mitigation against supply disruption.
- Take a note of the products that are turning into a commodity and whose sales are turning cost-driven. Reduce the production costs of these products on priority.
- Be clear about which lever to use for which product. Steady and regular products have lean inventory but a steady supply. For new products, create capacity on the run, that is, only when you are sure that the demand is increasing.
- Keep an eye on your market share as a percentage of overall market size. If there is any drop, get the feelers and act accordingly. Is the price a factor? Is quality a factor? Is customer service (order to delivery duration/ processes) a factor? Is availability a factor?

- Keep an eye on upcoming technology changes that can reduce production costs. Be the first to pick them and win the market as much as possible – first-mover advantage is very real in a cost-conscious industry that works on economies of scale.

Let us pivot our discussion from pharmaceuticals to healthcare delivery. Treatment at hospitals and performance of diagnostic tests, too, can end up cheaper if operational enhancements are thought through while designing them. For example, the design of treatments or diagnostic procedures rarely has a patient-centric focus. The procedures are usually more oriented toward healthcare provider who has both scarcity and information on his/her side. Anybody who had to repeat diagnostic tests to change their doctor might have experienced this aspect of healthcare provision. A few recommendations for this aspect are as follows:

- The use of technology to provide the health history of a patient and the way credit scores are maintained for borrowers is rare but can go a long way to reduce switching costs for patients if implemented and can be considered to be mandated by regulatory means to facilitate doctor portability.
- Doctors are the most loaded resources in the chain of healthcare delivery. Identifying those functions of doctors that can be performed by paramedic staff or can be re-engineered to reduce time and effort can go a long way. For example, the use of the 'theory of constraints' is not a radical idea in this aspect.

Bringing the factor of cost into the equation of healthcare provision might unlock affordable access to the bottom of the pyramid and thus is a significant opportunity in which operational improvements have to be thought through and implemented by both industry and regulators. This can lead to a future that is more equitable than the present and can be delivered even to those who didn't have healthcare access in the first place or have lost it on account of losing their economic relevance due to vagaries of growth.

Insurance - an important element of healthcare industry

To protect oneself from abrupt and random vagaries of debilitating health, health insurance over having individual 'medical treatment reserve savings' is an important way of handling medical expenses. It is interesting to deliberate here on the importance of ensuring broader health insurance coverage. Imagine an economy that has both healthy individuals and also those people, who are on the verge of falling sick, given either their age, their general health condition or their genes. If health insurance operates in a demand-supply market, the following would be the scenario:

- Those who are in the prime of their health would consider health insurance a burden on their money and would avoid buying it, since they don't see returns anytime soon.
- Those who are sick or on the verge of being sick would opt for health insurance.
- This situation would mean that insurance companies would be paying money to a bigger percentage of their insurance purchasers (since most will fall sick), and this, in turn, would mean that the companies would increase

the premium they are charging them to compensate for the high costs.
- Owing to high premium charges for insurance, far more people who are vulnerable would not be able to afford health insurance and will go without cover.

This would be a very inefficient market. Health insurance markets do have their kind of variations for tackling such situations. For example, some companies offer a gamut of coverage prices based on your age group and/or existing pre-medical conditions. Some need you to co-pay, that is, you would be required to bear a percentage of your medical bill along with the insurance company. So, if you are from the vulnerable group, a part of liability shifts to you and thus there is less need for a blanket increase of premiums. But these market-based responses are not in the best interest of the parties involved.

Imagine an alternate situation where buying insurance is made compulsory for everyone. In such a situation, due to high volumes and not all customers falling sick, the insurance company can afford to charge a lesser premium from the customers and still remain profitable. The healthy customers would cross-subsidize the weaker ones and when these healthy individuals will grow old and weak, there would be a new crop of healthy customers who would support them on account of universal coverage. Thus, for health insurance, some form of compulsion is a necessity to keep it functioning at lower costs. Thus, a regulatory intervention to ensure higher insurance coverage might be against the principle of the free-market but is probably preferable to laissez-faire.

Education:

Education is a rare feature among creatures of this world. Such an elaborate and collective system of training and transferring of knowledge is probably unique to us humans. It is one of the most important pillars that uphold culture in any society. It refines humans much more than any other activity undertaken by them. It has benefits and features that the economic mechanisms can't fully capture. A small part of these benefits is economic in nature - the part that trains people to undertake an occupation. Education impacts all aspects of society and, given the nature of current economic built-up, it impacts earning capacity much more than the previous eras when owning some means of production (an orchid, a bunch of cows, etc.) would have decided your economic fate.

Thus, the third industry being touched upon in this chapter is education. Though education is a vast subject and is much more than just being a mere industry, the following paragraphs focus only on the economic aspects of it, given the 'economical' scope of the book (pun intended!).

All the transactions have three associated costs - triangulation, transport and trust. Triangulation is the cost of finding the person who can provide the goods/service you need (if you are a consumer), and finding the person who is willing to pay for the good/service you supply (if you are a producer). Transport cost is the cost associated with moving the product/service from where it is produced to where it is needed. Trust cost is the cost for assuring the quality of a product and providing a guarantee that the product/service being supplied has the promised attributes and there is no actual or notional fraud involved.[12] Anything that eliminates, facilitates or reduces transactional costs is a platform. In ancient days, it used to be a bazaar. In current days, it is the app on your phone. Seen purely in these terms, schools and colleges and universities are one such platform that supposedly reduces two transactional costs: triangulation and trust. Companies need qualified individuals who are trained in the required skills. Instead of testing each individual for skills, the companies triangulate those who are from a particular educational institute – Why go around shopping for employees when we know that IIMs or Ivy Leagues have the bunch of brilliant individuals we need. Also, the educational institutes eliminate the costs associated with trust by providing companies an assurance that the individuals have a certain level of needed skills.

How efficient is the educational ecosystem in terms of this demand and supply performance? Are educational institutes performing well in their role as platforms? Do they upgrade themselves quick enough to be relevant to the needs of time? Do they impart skills at reasonable costs or are these costs turning unaffordable to an average person who wants to supply his/her services to companies? Is the trust being maintained by ensuring a sync between required and acquired skills?

When employers cannot trust that high school graduates know what they are supposed to, they start insisting on a college degree just to be sure of basic skills.[13] The problem of certification inflation (a big degree for a basic job) and a high premium for graduates from select institutes is an indicator of the inefficiency of our educational system.

The lack of relevance of skills is another problem. In most of the educational setups, students who spend formative years learning how to solve second-degree differential equations and matrices eventually would be required to use software to layout spreadsheets to code or to churn out profit scenarios and learn market nuances while managing sales and marketing events. After spending significant years and money at institutes, they find themselves well equipped to tackle a world that simply doesn't exist.

The speed of change of requirements at job, too, is becoming an issue that requires the attention of educationists. Learning a specific software might not assure you job security of five years leave aside the lifelong job guarantee that the previous generations had for their skills. New normal is turning into an old fable within months and the cutting edge solution is being called passé within quarters. Due to this constant churn, the individuals are experiencing the unease that one feels while driving a comfortable car, without GPS, in an unknown city.

Occupational licensing is another problem that contributes to the inefficiencies of the educational ecosystem. For example, in the USA, even barbers and manicurists are supposed to be licensed in most of the states.[14] In USA, licensing covered nearly 30% of the workforce in 2008 while it was around 5% in 1950.[15] The situation isn't significantly different in other economies.

Thus, there is a need and opportunity for entrepreneurs to come up with better 'platforms' for solving the transactional problem of skill supply.

A few ideas are mentioned below, but the canvas is still wide open for experimentation.

- Alma maters should be funded partially by a portion of (existing) income tax of their alumni for a fixed number of years. This can partially be in lieu of the funding that colleges receive from the government or the fees they charge from students. This would ensure skin in the game for the colleges. If their graduates earn better, colleges would get more income, and thus they would start upgrading themselves, collaborating with companies and keeping themselves relevant to ensure that their students are making money after graduating.

- Entrepreneurs have the opportunity in terms of providing offline and online relevant modules rather than long-term degrees for people so that they get right upskilling rather than costly degrees. A large number of online course platforms and hybrid models (with both online and offline training) are already in this domain, but there is a long way to go.
- A focus on enabling skills rather than tactical skills is the need of the hour in view of constant churn and shorter change cycles at organizations. Rather than teaching a particular version of a coding language, it is better to teach logic that is needed for talking to machines.
- Athletes develop their skill and muscle memory not by learning the nuances of their trade, but rather by repeatedly undergoing the drill that simulates their trade. A similar approach to education is extremely important, which, as of now, has very limited real-life-like simulations. Most internships and, to some extent, case studies simulate scaled-down versions of real-life experiences for students. Gamification and simulation by the innovative deployment of artificial intelligence and creation of physical and online sandboxes can be a good opportunity for edu-entrepreneurs.

The complexity of imparting education has grown exponentially. The nature of problems being tackled by the workforce has changed significantly over time. For example, the hand-axe and the mouse are both 'man-made'. But axe was made by a single person. Whereas, a mouse was created by the combined intelligence of multiple individuals. The person who assembled it in the factory did not know how to mine the plastic for it. At some point, human intelligence became collective and cumulative.[16]

Whether it is about planning civic amenities for cities that host millions or about use of artificial intelligence to manage global supply chains or whether it is about executing inter-planetary missions, the solutions and challenges that governments and organizations are currently grappling with have reached a scale that has become almost impossible for a single person or single field of science to solve. Even basic "research" that was glamorized by those lonely geniuses working in isolated basements is now all about large teams working together from multiple organizations and myriad geographies. (Remember the large hadron collider of CERN?)

Throughout history, humans have enabled more and more sophisticated solutions. But this "long walk to prosperity" has an inevitable side-effect - a single human being cannot master end to end anything that is being created as a solution. A surgeon, who is working on your heart, cannot be expected to smith out the scalpel that he is using to open you up!! Even the mundane, day-to-day jobs for retailers, manufacturers and programmers have turned very complex and involve scores of people and inputs from multiple countries.

Thus, the companies and governments now need, more than ever before, a workforce that has dual traits –the ability of specialization and the ability of cooperation. Craftsmen who believe in cooperation are used to empathizing with others and accept compromising local optima for the sake of larger good are the ideal people who would contribute to mankind's next wave of prosperity.

And these craftsmen are to be created from a generation for which individualism is "The Religion". TV remote ownership pacts with siblings is a regaling story that they heard from parents, but they never performed those pacts because they have all the entertainment needed on their "individual" gadgets. Teamwork and cooperation for them is a pointless virtue, which they at the most get to use in outdoor sports – and these sports are occupying a smaller portion of their activity pie with every passing day. Cooperation for them is a sign of weakness. Prioritizing others over themselves is senseless idealism.

What do we then have in store for governments, organizations and educationists going forward, with this mismatch of need and skills? The human resource managers and business leaders are the primary 'customers' of the products emerging from the education industry. Thus, a few 'user manual' tips for them are as under.

- "Purpose" is all the more important than before.

Indifference might be the defining trait of the current workforce, but passion too is rampant among them. In this generation that is called fickle, you can find individuals crazy enough to fight for animal property rights or patient enough to stand in long queues to get a new limited edition mobile phone. This generation is more of an explorer than a conqueror. It doesn't shy away from suffering inconvenience or bearing pain to get something. The only pre-requisite is that they should find "purpose" in it.

Thus, for any problem that a company is solving, it would be required to ensure that it hires a set of people who too believe in its bigger purpose, otherwise more than ever before, companies would end up with an indifferent workforce, who cannot be scared into obedience by their bosses and who would lose sense of purpose within milliseconds and would switch jobs!

We all keep scores to measure our success. For some, it's money; for others, it's fame or awards.[17] If what you achieve is no longer tied to "why" you set out to achieve it in the first place, it would create problems across the board.

Thus an important part of education should be ensuring team building and collaboration-related soft skills for grass root personnel as well. The army of program managers being hired these days to somehow miraculously contain the delay of projects has to be tinkered with for better results. The delays are more often than not due to the difficulty of collaboration rather than the lack of resources. These things need a set of soft skills that are to be explicitly taught but are conspicuously missing from our schooling and corporate training. A great opportunity for edu-entrepreneurs. Moving forward, organizations would need to pay special attention to these training needs, since ignoring them can only undermine their own potential.

- The next generation of solutions would be mostly achieved by using the existing tools for newer problems. Moving forward, it would be about, say, using artificial intelligence for hiring and training. Or, say, using RFID for carpooling. Or, say, deploying warehousing techniques for car parking. This would be a lot about creativity in seeing things in newer contexts. The workforce for sure needs to take cognizance of it and, for sure, collaboration would be one of the prime skillsets of the organizations that would accomplish these solutions. Trainings that focus on collaboration would be the next major innovation in education.

9

Lessons from Economic Disasters

Economists have their own ways of blowing things up. Economic turmoil has a mammoth impact on the lives of the masses. For example, consider two facts. Between 1929 and 1933, about 1/4th of the adult male population went out of a job.[1] Also, after the meltdown, the stock market didn't reach the levels of 1929 till 1958.[2]

The former of the above statements relate to income (return on labor) and the latter pertains to return on investment. Both the aspects of money generation got greatly impaired during Great Depression and the situation has been similar though to a different degree, during other economic slowdowns.

Another important point to note is that the years leading to the great depression of 1929 had their decent share of technological discoveries like airplanes and assembly lines, which had the potential for mass prosperity. Thus, it is difficult to claim that the depression of 1929 was on account of the sudden drop in technological discoveries or some unexpected loss of productivity. The slowdown that pushed a large portion of at least one generation into poverty was primarily due to wrong economic decisions and an incomplete understanding of economics coupled with some social events of the time.

9 Lessons from Economic Disasters

Learning lessons from these economic slowdowns can help us prevent them in in future.

The following paragraphs are an attempt to demystify a few important slowdowns.

The economy has initially been considered as a linear cause and effect linkage system with "ceteris paribus" (everything else remaining the same) as being the prime assumption of every theory. But, in more recent times, the complexity inherent in economics is being given its due. Economics is a complex and constant tussle between consumption, investment, lending, borrowing, taxation, employment, flow of money, exports, imports, collective psychology, and consumers' expectations about the future. The interaction between all these factors creates an equilibrium in the way the right balance between different parameters, like altitude, speed, lift, banking, fuel status, etc., keep an airplane flying. All the parameters of this mega airplane called economy should remain proportional and an abnormal increase/drop in any of them can bring down the airplane.

Slowdowns have been, at times, due to too much lending to people with no ability to payback (Recession of 2008), too much investing in a particular technology or industry (dotcom bubble of 2000), too much reliance on foreign investments with inefficient local financing (Asian financial crisis of 1997), wrong monetary policies (German inflation of 1920s) or a mix of these causes (Depression of 1929).

A few economic slowdowns, which would be brilliant case studies for understanding "why" and "how" of economics are:

1. Global Financial Crisis of 2008
2. Stock Market Bubble of 2000

3. Asian Crisis of 1997
4. The Indian Economic Crisis of 1991
5. The Great Depression of 1929

Many other economic crises have rocked the world. A few examples are Mexican Peso Crises of 1994, Debt crisis of 1982, Oil shock of 1973 in USA, Suez Crisis of 1956, German inflation of 1920s, the inflation in 16th century Europe due to the influx of silver, etc. But the need for brevity made me choose the above five. Nevertheless, all these slowdowns are equally good lessons and case studies in understanding what can go wrong with wrong economics.

Let's start with the Global Financial Crisis of 2008.

Financial Crisis of 2007-08

The Financial Crisis of 2007-08 was a classic case of "whatever can go wrong will go wrong". To put it briefly, this is what happened during the slowdown:

The "mass" home loans caught the fancy of common people. The banks, with this encouragement boosting them, disbursed loans with both hands - in many cases, to the people who didn't have full capacity to return the loans. The bankers were doing it because issuing loans got them revenue. People were taking loans because 1- It was making them feel rich and 2- the house prices were rising fast (there were more buyers since everyone was getting home loans) and they were hoping they would encash on these high prices. Basically, people were making a living by selling each other's houses.

As the situation progressed, the banks gave loans to Jack, Joe, Jane, Anne, Peter and 95 others but were a bit skeptical that all of them would return their loans. They "securitized" the loans; to put it simply, having given a loan of, say, $100

9 Lessons from Economic Disasters

to these hundred people (Jack, Joe, Jane...) at a 10% rate, they were expecting $11,000 at the end of the year (10,000 principal + 1000 interest). They sold certificates of this $10,000 to rich petro-sheikhs, the pension earning grandmas and other elders. They sold these certificates for, say, $10,100 and, at the end of the year, those who purchased the bonds would get $11,000. Banks earned $100 commission and also would free up their $10,000 to issue loans to 100 more people. Also, there was a risk management element to it: in case, say, two out of the hundred fail to pay back, banks wouldn't be in so much trouble. And the good thing is since certificates are bought by so many sheikhs and grandmas, the loss would get distributed across, and one person wouldn't face the heat. It is classic insurance. Rating agencies, seeing this awesome arrangement, gave upward of A ratings to these bonds, thus making them popular all across.

All this went fine until the house prices reached a ceiling and stopped rising further. And instead of just two persons defaulting, say, 50 persons out of those 100 defaulted - they were probably planning to repay by selling their homes at a higher price but that didn't work out. The banks fell short of money and they caught hold of the homes that have been bought by these defaulters and started selling them. This further deteriorated the price of the homes (more the houses on sale less people ready to buy) and the banks started feeling the heat. So, did those petro-sheikhs and grandmas!!

Thus, default in one corner of a country impacted people on the other side of the ocean. The whole situation created panic and people started pulling out money from investments and some big banks started collapsing. This resulted in a hold on spending, lost jobs and lost savings!!! This is an oversimplified meme of a very complex economic incident, but you got the gist.

This crisis has been extraordinarily dissected by RaghuramRajan in his book "Fault Lines". It is a must-read for those interested in 2007-08 crisis and macroeconomics at large.

What lesson does the crisis hold for posterity?

- Probably the biggest one is that issuing more money (through more credit or by printing more money) is not the remedy for every slowdown. Just ensuring more money in the hands of people and corporates can't ensure economic progress if the cause of the slowdown is, say,

1. Complex laws for hiring and firing people (poor labor laws)
2. Complex laws to start and end a business (incorporation laws and bankruptcy laws)
3. A too-slow-to-act government that is acting as a bottleneck on major decisions
4. A government that is issuing too many laws too fast and is causing unpredictability
5. Under-developed means of production

The above list (supply-side constraints) is not exhaustive, but, for sure, the availability of capital is just *one of the many* problems that hinders economic progress and pulling monetary (printing more/less money) or fiscal (increasing/decreasing tax) levers is not always the solution. But, governments tend to reach out to these levers because that is easy to do and shows quick results. But it would be just like accelerating a vehicle when it is in first gear. It would just cause sound and heat but not speed!!

9 Lessons from Economic Disasters

- The second lesson is about keeping the financial sector simple. Complex systems meant for mass consumption usually fail. The "models" used to provide ratings to the complex financial products were not able to fully measure the risk associated and thus rating agencies kept giving A+ to these products, while they were, in reality, border lining on Ponzi schemes. The economy should be driving the financial market but during the years leading to the 2008 crisis, it was the financial market that was driving economics.
- The third lesson is about inherent distorted incentives for economics and business players. One of the reasons rating agencies were giving high ratings to these financial products was because it made business sense for them to do so. The more products they rated A+, the more people bought those products and the more such new products get created, the more products they would have to rate and that is the very thing that brings them revenue. The bankers gave loans even to people with weak credit scores because issuing loan gets them revenue. If you are in the sales team and when your competitors are out there disbursing loans with both hands, it is difficult to sit back and show prudence- you can't resist dancing at a party where everyone is on the floor and the music is loud!!
- Almost every economic disaster is preceded by a spike in asset prices and 2007-08 was no different. As mentioned in previous lines, the house prices spiked on their way to 2007. The stock prices, too, had their time under the sun during these years. In the preceding five years to July 31, 2007, on an average annualized basis, most of the world's equity markets delivered double-digit returns.

[3] Basically, there was a disproportionate rise in asset prices. This happened maybe because people had easy access to money: banks giving loans easily, central banks reducing interest rates so that people use their money instead of keeping them in banks and governments taking more loans from central banks to spend on populist schemes. More money chasing the same goods and services causes a disproportionate rise in prices and results in a burst when prices reach a ceiling.

Dotcom Bubble of 2000

The next economic issue to be discussed is the stock price build-up of the late 1990s and early 2000s, during which, the value of any stock that had dotcom at its end skyrocketed. From that sky of 2000, the stocks had a free fall, reaching bottom in 2002. Nasdaq peaked on March 10, 2000, at 5,048.62. It didn't reach this level again till March 2015. Comparing the March 2000 peak, to the trough of October 9, 2002, the Nasdaq lost nearly 80 percent of its value.[4]

This severe drop had a terrible effect on everyday Jack and Joe, who were one of the biggest investors at the time of the peaking of the stocks.

Here is how the wisdom of those days worked:

- Create a company, call it internet-company and have ".com" at its end.
- Don't care about profits
- The hype that the solution being created will change the face of..... (fill your blank here) industry.

9 Lessons from Economic Disasters

- Hope that revenue would be mostly generated by advertisements and, in some cases, by taking a percentage from the partners whose transactions you are facilitating
- Put all the capital you got to advertise your way to recognition

The idea seemed brilliant, except for the fact that most of the founders of these companies and their backers had some version of 'pro-innovation bias'. The value that those companies were providing was not on par with the costs involved, the ecosystem of adjacent industries (say, banking sector) was not yet ready and customer adaptation, which has its own rhythm and cycle, was totally presumed as given.

The success of any economic product/solution is a balance of multiple factors as shown in the figure below:

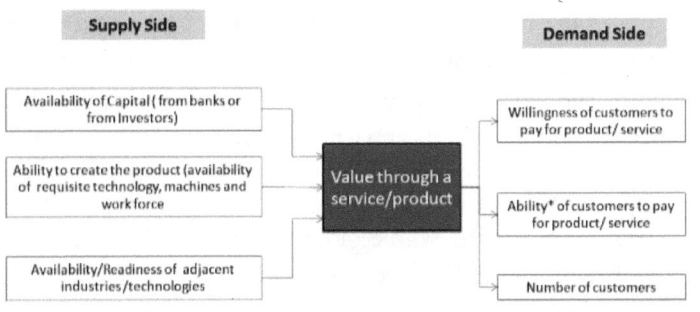

* To understand difference between willingness and ability consider my example ☺, I consider Ferrari to be a great car and am willing to pay for the value it provides me, but the problem is I don't have "ability" to do so!!

In the case of dotcom companies of the late nineties, the industry was flush with capital due to the excitement around the technology but the other factors were not yet ready. So, putting money into a system that is otherwise not ready, as told previously, is like accelerating your car in low gear. It would only make sound but won't pick up speed as it would in top gear.

More money was chasing those limited number of dotcom companies and thus their stock prices inflated, though there was very less revenue and even lesser profits.

Thus, the most important lesson from the crisis of 2000 was:

Not every economic problem can be solved by putting in more money. Some problems (from macro/microeconomics) are due to, say, inadequate demand or half-baked technology or, say, the inability of the government to eliminate regulations that are hindering business creation.

1997-1998 East Asian Crisis

The 1997-98 crisis is yet another case study from which a few nuggets of wisdom can be extracted. Let us take our timemachine to a typical East Asian country of 1995. Once we land, the native learned man, who has seen it all in his country would narrate its story to us in these simple words:

- The world started believing in our ability to create prosperity for the whole globe and invested money left, right and center. To give a sense of numbers, investment, as a percentage of GDP across Korea, Malaysia and Thailand, increased from 29% in 1988 to 42% in 1996.[5]
- The ambitious manufacturers who lived around here started dreaming of silicon-wafer fabrication facilities, petrochemical complexes and integrated steel plants.
- Initially, the government was directing the investment funds, to decide who gets how much money for investing in big plants.

9 Lessons from Economic Disasters

- But, as investment started coming in for complex technologies, governments stopped directing money allocation and the responsibility started coming to bankers who lived around here.
- The banks in those times (and probably even now) depended on long-term relationships with local corporations. And to understand, if the corporations had the ability to pay back, the bankers used to rely on their conversations with corporate honchos during cocktail dinners rather than on those raw numbers that companies used to publish.
- Such relationship-based credit lending was inefficient, for it was slow, was more subjective and couldn't be scaled. Result was under-developed domestic banks.
- Coupled with it, the foreign funds that were coming were relying on banks for their investments, the reason being that these banks had relatively better local understanding and the foreign funds didn't want to rely on those raw numbers (the way local banks didn't want to).
- Also, foreign funds understood that the governments will come to the rescue of local banks in case of failure.
- Things kept going fine, but two things happened and triggered trouble:
  - The local companies, due to a lack of technical know-how, started getting into trouble. The construction of fabrication facilities and petrochemical complexes started facing project delays and overshooting costs as the companies kept stumbling during their walk on the learning curve.
  - Around the same time, the Japanese Yen fell in value and thus their exports became cheap (they were getting more Yens for the same one dollar and used

it to create more products). The foreign funds started flying to Japan because they loved the Japanese quality, which, as an icing on the cake, was cheaper now.

- The foreign funds wanted their money back, but local companies, couldn't pay while staring at their failed projects. This triggered issues for funds the world over as they were not getting their money back. The investors started clamoring for their pound of flesh. Eventually, IMF intervened and imposed quite a few restrictions on my country, which is a story for another day!!! People lost a lot of their money and things were never the same again.

The crisis was largely a result of corporate over-investment in manufacturing and real estate.[6] We cannot help but go back to the diagram shown in previous paragraphs. The Asian crisis was probably that of "supply-side" in which the "ability to create product" of the above diagram couldn't keep pace with the "availability of capital".

Lessons for us:

- Not all problems could be solved by infusing more money (again)
- The ability to produce comes a bit gradually, so does the ability to spend and this speed should be considered while solving an economic slowdown
- Keep an eye on both supply-side and demand-side while pushing for economic progress

The 1991 Balance of Payment Crisis in India

India faced an economic problem in the early days of 1991, which escalated to the extent that the country was staring

9 Lessons from Economic Disasters

at the possibility of payment default to foreign lenders. The possibility was eventually mitigated and subsequently evaded by extraordinary reforms that were taken in July of that year. Those reforms apart, from dodging the crisis, pivoted the country on a much different path, by dismantling the controls that the government had on means of production.

To understand what the problem was, how it grew so big and how it was evaded, let us first understand how a country's economy interacts with the international economy.

Any country, inside its boundaries, deals in its own currency. But, for dealing, with others outside the country, it either needs the currency of the country with which it is dealing (say, buying petrol from Iran in the Iranian Rial) or it needs a currency that is universally accepted (read US dollars). Since the country cannot mint/print these outside currencies, the following are the ways in which it can get the outside currencies:

1. By selling products/services to other countries and taking payment in outside currency (this is export)
2. By allowing outsiders to invest within its boundaries. They will bring their currency, convert it into local currency and then invest to create production plants/offices locally or buy shares of local firms (this is FDI or FII)
3. By receiving remittances from those locals, who are living outside the country and making money and sending it back to their families
4. Through loans from outside the country
5. Through aid from outside the country

The foreign currency, received from the above five options is used for the following:

1. To buy stuff from outside the country (this is called imports)
2. To pay back foreign lenders

What happened during 1991:

Leading to the year 1991, a few of the above seven items (5+2) gradually started moving in an undesirable direction and then they culminated in a full-blown crisis eventually. Here are a few pointers:

1. **Exports**: Before the year 1991, for its local factories, India had a lot of restrictions, even in terms of, say, the size of the production plant and the number of units the plant can produce, etc. This lead to severe inefficiencies for exporters who had to take production decisions not based on business sense but rather based on political and bureaucratic diktats. That eventually meant high-cost exports with compromised quality. The exports dwindled as no outside country wanted this lose-lose deal. The foreign currency turned into a trickle via this option.
2. **FDI/FII**: The country had restrictions on foreign investors bringing in their money to establish manufacturing plants or buy shares of local productions. The zeitgeist of the time was that foreign money, when it would come along with foreign technology, would overwhelm the fledgling local industry and smother it to death. But the side effect of these restrictions was an inefficient local market and meager foreign investment. Very less foreign currency came in via this route.

9 Lessons from Economic Disasters

3. **Imports**: The geopolitical turmoil in the Middle East during the last few months of 1990 led to a sharp rise in oil prices. Oil was the biggest contributor to the import bill at that time (even now it is). This sharp rise practically meant a sudden need for more foreign currency to cater to domestic oil demand.
4. **External Debt:** India's share of external debt in national income went up from 17.7% to 24.5% from 1980 to 1989.[7]

These factors evaporated the foreign funds available to India and subsequently led to a desperate situation. By June 1991, India had very less foreign reserves to cater to its imports. The situation was so dire that India had to airlift 20 tons of gold in May 1991. In March, the country banned many imports. Again, in July 1991, India pledged almost 47 tonnes of gold to the Bank of England to secure emergency funds.[8]

These symbolic events shook the whole country and eventually pushed the regime out to take measures.

The major reforms undertaken along with the timeline are listed below:

1. **1 July 1991:** Government devalued rupee by around 9%.[9]
2. **3 July 1991**: Rupee further devalued by 11%.[10] This devaluation meant more rupees being earned by exporters for the same quantity of export sales. This incentivized exports and made people put in money to export and thus bring in foreign cash.
3. **3 July 1991:** The export-related subsidies were abolished (Cash Compensatory System).[11] This meant, that those exporters who were inefficient but were surviving on government subsidies had to mend their ways or close

down the shop due to market forces. This led to better quality exports from India.

4. **24 July 1991:** Via the historic budget, the fiscal deficit was reduced from the high of 8.2% to about 6%.[12] A fiscal deficit is nothing but the difference between revenue and income of the government. Reducing spending meant taking a lower loan.

5. **September 1991**: Government-issued ordinance removing restrictions on capacity expansion and merger and acquisition that were closely controlled by the Monopolies and Restrictive Trade Practices Act of 1969.[13]

The above measures, partly taken in desperation and partly with a belief in an"idea whose time has come", pivoted India onto a much stronger path and turned it into the service sector powerhouse it is today. New sectors and new faces emerged within a decade. The 1990s had predominantly infrastructure and steel defining the business face of the country. But, in 2000s, it was the firms in information technology and services that were the leading companies.[14]

What are the lessons for us in this historic episode:

- Biggest and most important lesson: Too much interference by government, even with good intentions, in matters of business is not good. Creating a level playing field and leaving it to market forces is the way rather than the government defining what and how of production.
- The government's decisions have after-effects that go on for decades and, in some cases, centuries.

The Great Depression of 1929

The 1929 Depression was probably the mother of all economic crises. From 1929 to 1933, real GDP in the major economies fell by over 25 percent and a quarter of the adult male population lost jobs, there was a sharp fall in commodity prices, consumer prices declined by 30% and wages went down by a third. Bank credit got reduced by 40% in the US.[15]

A few important pointers:

- The period leading to these years was not that of low or no technological development. There was mass production of cars, invention of new chemicals, proliferation of radios, commercialization of airplane industry, etc. These technologies had the potential for mass prosperity, but the economics of the time let them down!!
- It was not a single crisis, rather it was a bundle of crises that fed upon each other.

It probably began with the end of World War 1. A few of the most important incidents along with the timelines, during those seminal years, are mentioned below in an attempt to simplify the complex disaster that "Great Depression" was.

- **Europe 1923**: The value of Germany's currency went into a free fall. The German government, after the defeat of WWI, started unabated printing of its currency to pay back the money it borrowed from its people in the form of "war bonds" and to pay the workers who were not even working (rather protesting against France occupation of Ruhr region). There was a lot of money in the hands of the people, but no matching production in war-torn Germany. A lot of money was chasing the same, or rather, lesser products and services and thus the prices sky-rocketed. To get a feel, consider the fact that, by August 1923, a dollar was worth 620,000 German marks, and by early November 1923, 630 billion. Germany was one of the biggest economies of Europe (and thus the world), and thus, the failure of its monetary system sent a shock across the whole Europe and impacted the world economy already limping post World War 1.

- **Europe 1928:** Germany was on brink of bankruptcy. Another problem of the time was that the currencies were linked with gold. The amount of money in circulation was linked with the amount of gold the country dugout and not to the economic activity of the country. This proved to be a severe straight jacket.
- **US 1928**: Share prices started to break free from economic reality. Starting summer of 1928, within 15 months, Dow went from 200 to 380. Around the same time, industrial production was falling at an annualized rate of 45%. Shares of "new technologies", like aluminum, airplanes and radio, were skyrocketing. This infatuation with "new tech" has a parallel in the 2000 dotcom bubble. As the American money in Europe was being sucked back into a few US stocks, the (WWI) war-torn Europe, in need of money, got one more push towards abyss (The recession of Germany due to the shortage of foreign money has a parallel in the Mexican peso crisis of 1994).
- **Europe 1929**: To slow this flight of money, European banks raised their interest rates (so that people keep

9 Lessons from Economic Disasters

money in the local market in hopes of better returns). This, in turn, sucked money from local markets further (People, rather than investing or consuming, deposited their money in banks). A worldwide slowdown was approaching. But the US stocks continued their blissful hurtle.

- **US Oct 1929:** On October 29, 1929, now known as Black Tuesday, a sell-off started. It was huge. Over just two days, October 28 and 29, the Dow lost close to 25%. By November 13, it was at 198, down 45% in two months.

- **1929-30**: The bubble burst in the US resulted in shrinking US demand for European goods. Also, in June 1930, Smoot Hawley Act needed that Europe can get American products only in exchange for gold. This led to a further shortage of gold in Europe, on which most of its currencies were pegged. Also, during the same time, France was (relatively) a bright spot in Europe. Capital, and thus, gold was flowing to France in bulk. The United States and France, between them, held 60% of the world's gold, and it wasn't circulating[16] Economies needed more money in the system, but remaining pegged to gold, they had lesser money. The world slowdown turned full-blown. Multiple factors like Germany nearing a default, the gold shortage, falling commodity prices, the US exchanges' rise and a weak sterling contributed in their own ways.

- **1931-33**: Bank failures came in waves. The first, in 1930, began with bank runs in agricultural states, such as Arkansas, Illinois and Missouri. A total of 1,350 banks failed that year. External pressure worsened the US domestic worries. As Britain dumped the Gold Standard, its exchange rate dropped, putting pressure on American exporters. There were banking panics in Austria and Germany. As public confidence evaporated, Americans began to hoard currency. Nearly 11,000 banks had failed between 1929 and 1933, and the money supply dropped by over 30%.

These failures have a parallel in the recession of 2007. But in 2007, things were responded to in a much better manner. In 1931, Fed didn't respond to these failures and believed in laissez-faire, whereas, in 2007, central banks all around the world propped up the system by injecting a huge amount of credits.

Lessons:

- The hyper-concentration of money in a few stocks. The madness around the new technologies was so much that, even at its peak, Dow was roaring not because of overall stocks rise, but rather due to those few shares that held a mirage in name of promise. On Sep 3, 1929, the day the Dow peaked; only about 2% on the New York Stock Exchange attained all-time highs.[17] The mistake was repeated in 2000 for dotcom shares. It is important that we remember this lesson when the promise of autonomous robots, renewable bodies, interplanetary travel or human teleportation is made to us in the coming century.
- The biggest lesson that the world learnt was that once slowdown occurs, the governments should step in the kick-start economy by stepping up their spending and credit infusion. This idea was given by Maynard Keynes

and because the economists world over remembered this lesson, the 2007-08 recession wasn't as sticky as the one in 1929.
- Another important legacy of 1929 was the discarding of the gold standard. The circulation of money in an economy should be dependent upon the level of economic activity in a country, not on the quantity of a particular being mined. This was a rather simple idea, but it took a crisis for humanity to fathom it.

Is it Different This Time?

As the book is being authored in 2022, the share prices across the world have seen an extraordinary rise, subsequent to the fall experienced during 2020, mainly due to lockdowns and bans imposed during 2020 on account of COVID-19. Though the overall economy got impacted during 2020, but the equity indices across the world tell an opposite story. Will this impacted economy coupled with sky-high equity prices lead to an economic slowdown as we move forward? It is difficult to be predicted accurately as was the case with all the other economic slowdowns, but it is an interesting case that readers should try to study and understand.

10

Shape and Form of Different Industries

Having seen examples of the slowdown of overall economies, let us take a step back and try to look at the individual industries in an economy.

Economies are like ecosystems. The way an ecosystem has different species classified into interrelated biological families and food chains, an economy, too, has different industries that feed and prosper off each other. An ecosystem has different kinds of species. Some species, say, ants would be high in number, but smaller in size while some species are huge in size but fewer in numbers, like whales. All of them are dependent upon each other, some intimately, while others vaguely. In an economy, too, there are some industries, say, the restaurant industry, that have a high number of small players, while some others, say, the airplane manufacturing industry, have few large players – and these industries, too, are dependent upon each other in complex and myriad ways. Different ecosystems are different in terms of the species they are home to. Say, for example, Kangaroos exist only in Australia due to factors specific to the Australian biological ecosystem. Economies, too, are significantly different in different countries and are highly influenced by country-specific factors, like the size of the population, level of education, geographic factors (you can't sell skiing gear in the Sahara desert), regulatory factors, etc. Economists try to classify industries the way biologists try to classify species. And, at times, they find it difficult to classify an industry the way biologists too get confused - the economics, too, has its duck-billed platypuses.

While the comparison between economics and the biological ecosystem is good to point to the complexity of economics, it might be an insufficient comparison to bring home the point around its speed and dynamics. Ecosystems progress through evolution, whereas economics progresses both through evolution and revolution. At times, industries change their form and shape within a decade, whereas species usually take far more time.

Studying an industry is a prerequisite to managing it effectively and thus governments who are supposed to find the right path between laissez-faire and complete control try to classify as well as understand industries. The investors, too, need to predict the emergence of new industries and decipher the survival of old ones. Usually, industries undergo change on account of changing needs of their customers and also on account of changing adjacent industries. Changes in an unrelated industry, too, impacts an industry in many cases – for example, when information technology led to riches in Silicon Valley, the real estate industry of the region found a big boom. As a matter of fact, information technology developments in Silicon Valley lead to the creation of a humming IT export industry in India and the real estate of Indian cities of Bangalore and Hyderabad too got a slice of the pie of prosperity- though the coders of California and cement vendors of Hyderabad don't seem to be connected in any manner whatsoever.

Part – I: Macroeconomics

This chapter wouldn't be dissecting the anatomy of individual industries. Rather, it would be attempting at pointing out some factors and influences that affect the formation of industries.

Let us attempt to understand why some industries undergo cycles of heavy boom and bust every few years. For example, say, steel industry or airline industry undergoes booms and bust cycles once in a while. So, does the container shipping industry. But that doesn't usually happen to a group of fashion retailers!! The answer may be that these industries have a high capital need and thus attract speculation. But, the petroleum refining industry, with a capital need as high as that of airlines, doesn't undergo such cycles so often. Why is it so? The following paragraphs are an attempt to answer the same. The idea being proposed in these paragraphs isn't peer-reviewed. It is just a speculative discussion to decipher the probable cause of booms and busts.

Grouping industries in accordance with "capital needs vs demand fluctuations" might give an answer to the booms and busts cycle of different industries.

The industries would get grouped into four quadrants with this classification as shown in the figure below.

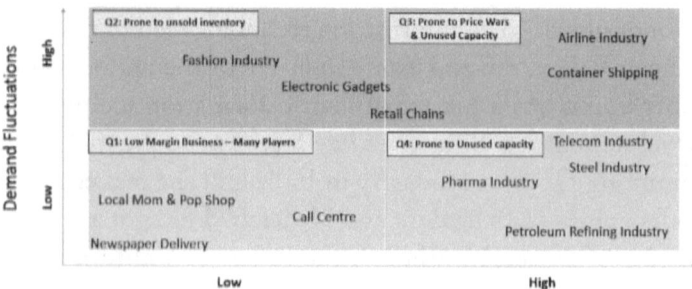

Fixed Cost as percentage of Total Cost

10 Shape and Form of Different Industries

Q1 – Industries with low fixed costs and low demand fluctuations:

Have you ever seen a newspaper delivery person declaring bankruptcy? No, it doesn't happen because in such an industry the need for money to initiate a business is very less. Thus, if there is a slowdown, the players make an exit, but there won't be any shells left with huge sunk costs. Such an industry will be a low-margin business with no mad rush to earn profit with huge asset buildup. Newspaper delivery agencies, mom and pop retail stores, etc. are examples of such an industry.

Q2 – Industries with high demand fluctuations but lesser capital needs:

These industries when they undergo a demand fall end up with high inventories but don't go bust as frequently as industries in Quadrant 3, since they won't have large unused machinery lying idle. They may lay off employees but will not be sitting with huge fixed costs. Such industries tend to have "end of season" sales to clear their inventories. For example, mobile handset retailers and fashion and sport apparel retailers.

Q3 – Industries with high demand fluctuation and high capital needs:

Here, the fixed costs are extremely high and demand is fluctuating. Whenever there is a sharp demand fall in this industry, to utilize their available capacity in which they have invested large amounts (airline has already paid for a plane whether it is flying or not), the players start reducing prices to attract customers. This situation creates a scenario, where there is falling demand and falling prices – a perfect recipe to go bust. Airline industry, container shipping, etc., are such industries. These industries tend to be commodity industries but with relatively higher fixed investments (differentiating your product through a brand is very difficult).

Q4 – Industries with low demand fluctuations but with high capital needs:

These industries need initial capital to start a business. The demand fluctuations in such industries are lesser making it easier to predict the capacity and capital needed. Players don't indulge in price wars to attract customers since there is no sharp fall/fluctuation in demand. Such industries, though at times end up with excess capacity, followed by industry consolidation, but homicidal price cuts don't usually happen here. Petroleum, pharma, and steel industries are some examples.

This brings us to the question as to why do industry players invest in excess capacity for Q3 and Q4 industries when they know that they might end up with a supply capacity with no demand to balance it – The answer is "time lapse between investments to cash-flow". Imagine that you are a container shipper. You would see that there is a lot of demand for shipping due to (say) Chinese exports. You order a new ship. So, does your neighbor, which you don't know about. End of the year, both you and your neighbor (and a few similar neighbors) have brand new ships that you thought you will rent for $500 per container. But given that so many ships are in the market (supply capacity) and the demand is the same or fluctuating, the scenario completely changes. The per-container rent falls to $200, which probably won't be sufficient for you to even cater the loan that you took to buy the new ship. What would happen? You would reduce the price to attract customers since you already have a heavy sunk cost and you would like to retrieve it. And when that doesn't save you, the

10 Shape and Form of Different Industries

ship would be put up for sale and so would all the other ships by the neighbors, who, as a matter of fact, took a heavy loan to build new ships. The industry goes bust due to this. Ships go to a scrapeyard and, eventually, in the year after that, there is a shortage of ships and the cycle repeats itself!!!

Closely associated with this cycle of investment boom and bust in industries is the aspect of consolidation and monopoly. Many firms have changed the texture of their industries. They leveraged economies of scale, higher efficiency and cheaper availability of capital in previously disorganized industries and consolidated them by buying out smaller players. This, at times, led to better service for customers, but many times, once the a player grows too big, it starts monopolistic behavior and tries to charge extremely high prices on account of its sheer size and lack of alternatives. Similarly, many times, the sellers of an industry collude with each other and agree on pricing so that the customer is forced to pay a higher price due to a lack of alternatives. Such behavior is considered illegal since it leads to the abuse of power by one player in the market over others. The laws pertaining to regulation of such behavior and tackling monopolistic firms are called Anti-Trust laws. These laws are evoked to ratify any merger or acquisition happening in any industry since mergers might lead to the creation of mega players, which, later, can dominate the market due to a lack of alternatives.

Industries are a group of firms and, as pointed out earlier, they have their own duck-billed platypuses, the firms that operate in seemingly different industries. The motives of companies, their performance, their capacity development strategies and the development of competitive advantage all play an important role in the performance of these companies, and thus, overall industries.

Part – II

Business Management, Finance and Company Operations

This section covers topics around company operations, financial analysis and business management.

A major portion of this section pertains to understanding the logic behind financial statements, their inter-relations and their influence on profits as well as operations of companies. If you are expecting this section to be a refresher on 'how to' of P&L or balance sheet, then you would be disappointed. Rather, this section is more of a debrief around the 'why' of the financial statements and is targeted at mid-level managers who want to strengthen their understanding of company operations and want the learning around practical implications of financial statements. It also might be helpful to students who want to understand the 'why' aspect of accounting. Though it is not a prerequisite, it is advisable that the reader brushes his/her 'how to' around financial statements before reading this section.

11

Introduction to Financial Statements

This chapter explains why three statements are used to depict the financial health of an organization. It also explains the overall structure of the financial statements without dwelling on their technicalities and 'how to create'. If you have studied basic accounting as a 'necessary evil' by mugging up "debit what comes in- credit what goes out" and by meticulously subtracting depreciation from the asset value without understanding the reason and logic behind doing so, this chapter might help you a bit.

Why do we have three financial statements: balance sheet, income statement & cash flow?

The first doubt we get while studying accounting is why do we need three statements? Won't it be sufficient to have one statement in which all the incomes and expenses are listed?

To understand this, let us first see how we run a business. We arrange some money (ourselves, from partners/investors and from loans), then we buy stuff to run the company and then sell our products. We make a profit that we share between ourselves, our investors/partners and creditors. I have depicted the same in the diagram below.

Part – II: Business Management, Finance and Company Operations

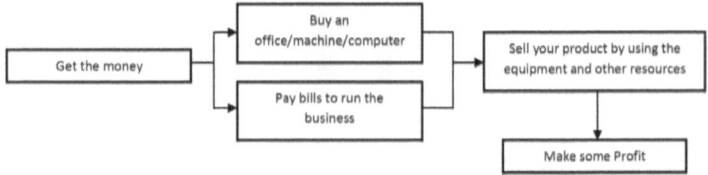

If you want to sell your company or, say, want to get some loan or want to add new partners, the first thing the new partners or lenders would ask you is what all is there in your factory of which I am purchasing a share or against what equipment/assets am I lending?

If you have a single statement with a list of all your expenses, then you would be required to separate out all the expenses you made to purchase the equipment. In other words, you make a list of assets. Also, you would be required to show all pending payments and loan bills the company has on it. In other words, you would need a list of liabilities. And assets minus the liabilities will be considered as the book value of your company. Thus,

Asset - Liabilities = Equity

This is the famous balance sheet equation. The balance sheet is the statement of the status of the company on a particular day. The status of the company would change with, say, more liabilities or more equipment with every passing day. Thus, the balance sheet has the heading "Balance sheet as on....".

The other point is that you don't purchase big machinery every time you sell the products. To know whether you are making a profit, you would be required to list all your day-to-day expenses and revenues together without including big machinery. This is where the income statement comes in handy. The income statement is for a particular period....

usually a year. It reads "Expenses and Income for the duration of ...."

Thus, essentially, these two statements complement each other.

Things that appear in both statements:

Suppose you purchase a machine for your factory and its cost is more or less equal to this year's revenue. It will be used for the next fifteen years. If you subtract the price of the machine from your revenue, in the income statement, this year's income statement will show a heavy loss. And next year's income statement will show a high profit compared to this year. Thus, we will see heavy fluctuations in profit percentage year on year. To avoid this, you divide the cost of your asset over 15 years. And subtract it every year. This small value that is annually subtracted is called depreciation. Also, since the market value of the asset deteriorates year on year, the same value of depreciation is subtracted from the asset side of the balance sheet at end of each year. Thus, the depreciation appears both in the income statement and in the balance sheet.

There are a few more things that appear in both the income statement and balance sheet. For example, the money spent on purchasing raw materials is shown in the "cost of goods sold". The same thing comes on the asset side as "inventory".

Cash Flow:

Let's now understand what is cash flow statement and how it is different compared to a profit and loss statement through a simple example. Imagine that you run a company.

Part – II: Business Management, Finance and Company Operations

Consider that you have non-fixed expenses, like raw material, packaging, etc. (technically called cost of goods sold (COGS)) at 60% of your sales and fixed operating expenses (like salaries, factory rent, etc.) of $10000. And suppose you have $10000 in your account in form of cash at the start of January. Your sales are at $50,000. According to P & L, during the month of January you made a profit of $10,000, as shown in the following figure.

Income from revenue (A)	$50,000
Expenses	
Variable expense (COGS) (B)	$30,000
Fixed expense (C)	$10,000
Profit ((A)-(B)-(C))	**$10,000**

But to add a dose of practicality, let us imagine that there are two clauses:

1. You pay your suppliers after 30 days (raw material and packaging suppliers) – a monthly payment cycle
2. Your customers pay you after 60 days

Now, let us see your cash situation for the next three months:

During January:

- You have to pay $10000 operating expenses. You use $10000 in your bank account.
- You have receivables of $50000 and payables of $30000 and neither of the two have been transacted yet.
- Now you are left with zero cash with you. The details are depicted in the following table.

11 Introduction to Financial Statements

	January
Cash you have	
Bank account	$10,000
Payment from customers	$0
Cash you need to pay	
Fixed expense (salaries, factory rent)	$10,000
To be paid to suppliers	$0
Net remaining at month-end	
To be paid – Received	$10,000 – $10,000
	$0

During February:

- You have to pay $10000 operating expenses. You don't have cash. Never mind. You are making profit. So, don't worry.
- You have to pay $30000 (Jan COGS – 30 days are over).
- You have a total need of $40000 cash ($10,000+ $30,000) and you have none. You are in trouble, even though you are making profit.

	January	February
Cash you have		
Bank account	$10,000	$0
Payment from customers	$0	$0
Cash you need to pay		
Fixed expense (salaries, factory rent)	$10,000	$10,000
To be paid to suppliers	$0	$30,000

Part – II: Business Management, Finance and Company Operations

Net remaining at month-end		
Received - To be paid	$10,000 – $10,000	$0 – $40,000
	$0	–$40,000

Let us hope that you survived the month by convincing the suppliers and your landlord that you are making profits and request them to provide you some time.

During March:

- You have finally received $50000 from your sales in January (60 days are over).
- You now paid $40,000 that you were supposed to pay last month. You hope this month you are not going to face a problem. You have 10,000 spare cash now (50k – 40k).
- But you have to pay ($10,000 + $30,000) this month as well. So, you again have a cash hole of $40,000.

	January	February	March
Cash you have			
Bank account	$10,000	$0	$0
From customers	$0	$0	$50,000
Cash you need to pay			
Fixed expense (salaries, factory rent)	$10,000	$10,000	$10,000 +$10,000 (Feb)
To be paid to suppliers	$0	$30,000	$30,000 +$30,000 (Feb)
Net remaining at month-end			
Received - To be paid	$10,000- $10,000	$0 – $40,000	$50,000 – $80,000
	$0	–$40,000	–$30,000

11 Introduction to Financial Statements

Do you see what is happening here? Though you are making a profit, just because of shortage of capital for day-to-day working, you may face hassles to run the business. Cash is an important entity and P&L alone is not sufficient to provide a true picture of its availability with the company. The cash flow statement provides that detail.

From this example, you can drive a lesson that if the payment cycle is reversed, that is, if we can get to pay to suppliers after 60 days and receive payment from customers within 30 days, we would be very comfortable in handling the cash. But not all businesses get such a lucky business scenario. But many businesses do have such a cash cycle. For example, we pay upfront to online retailers when we buy something off their website. But they usually pay their suppliers at the end of the month. This business model makes them very comfortable in terms of cash management.

12

Accounting Discretion Available in Financial Statements

Having understood the basics of the three financial statements, let us probe them a bit further.

For most retail investors, a financial statement is only about the top-line (revenue) and the bottom-line (profit). But analyzing a financial statement is more about reading between these two lines!!

While comparing companies for their financial health, one should be cognizant of the fact that companies do have slight discretion in terms of deciding the finer details of the way they record and report their finances. The representative examples provided in the following paragraphs are meant to drive this point home. There are some controls on these finer details reported by companies through auditing and regulations but, nevertheless, it is true that footnotes of the annual reports and 10Ks deserve a lot more attention than we generally provide them.

Altering the duration of depreciation:

In the previous chapter, we have understood that expense around the purchase of an asset is distributed over some years, and each year, the proportionate portion of asset spend (capital expense) is shown as a cost in the profit and loss statement and is called depreciation.

Imagine that you bought such an asset, say, a truck worth $50,000 for your firm and it is obviously a capital investment. You have decided to depreciate it over ten years. So, what do you do? You decrease $5000 (50,000/10 years) every year from profit (Though depreciation is not equally divided between years, we can consider so for the purpose at hand). Just imagine that this year you, say, in the footnote that trucks survive for twenty years, not ten, and thus, you are depreciating $2500 ($50,000/20) every year from this year on. Voila!! This year, your profit is higher by $2,500 compared to the previous year without any change in operations. So, if you are comparing two companies who have high capital expenditure and, thus, high depreciation, then it would be best to compare their footnotes to ascertain whether their depreciation policies are comparable or do they need adjustment for a fair comparison.

Adjusting capital expenditure:

Let's alter our previous example slightly. If you own a logistics firm and you purchased a truck for $50,000. You may say it is meant to run your operations.... right? So it comes under your operational expenses. Now, next year you bought a new truck and you argue that it is meant to expand your capacity so it should be capital expenditure. So, this time, your operational expense is less by $50,000 (they are on the balance sheet as a capital expense) and thus your "Gross Profit" will not be affected now. In the real world, such swings are difficult due to regulatory restrictions, but not inexistent. At times, management, just to show higher profits, move their operating expense into the balance sheet as capital expenditure and they show higher profit without doing anything.

Assets vs Goodwill:

Suppose you are purchasing a company. You valued it. Accounted all assets and arrived at $300,000. But the owner of the company asked for $500,000 and you purchased it at $500,000 because you believe it is in a growing industry and has an amazing customer base and you would more than compensate for the additional $200,000 through future profits. Now, your balance sheet is increased by an asset worth $500,000… but wait, it has physical assets worth only $300,000. The remaining $200,000 would be shown as "goodwill".

Now is the catch. The $300,000 of assets will get depreciated over, say, 10 years and thus your "net profit" will get reduced by $30,000 per year (that is, your profits are down by $30,000 every year). But goodwill is not generally depreciated (The appropriate word is amortization). So, that $200,000 will not at all affect your P&L statement. So, when you buy a company, you will have an incentive to undervalue the $300,000 (assets) and overvalue the $200,000 (goodwill). If you show that you have paid $100,000 in assets and $400,000 in goodwill your annual depreciation is just $10,000 and you have higher profits compared to the earlier situation!!!

'Expense' deducted from surplus:

Before getting into the details of this example, let's first understand the term 'surplus' or 'retained earning'.

What does a company do at the end of a year with its 'earnings'/profits? It partially gives them away to the shareholders in the form of dividends and partially keeps them

12 Accounting Discretion Available in Financial Statements

with itself in the form of 'retained earnings/surplus' (there is a slight difference between surplus and retained earnings, but for the purpose at hand, we can use them interchangeably). So, companies usually have a buffer of earnings with them accumulated over years that can be used either for further investments used on a rainy day.

But some companies, even on a normal day, subtract certain expenses from 'surplus' rather than subtracting them from operational income. This way, they can make profits look healthy without much effort since people rarely compare the current year's surplus with that of the previous year.

One can check the authenticity of an income statement by looking at the surplus that has been reported by the company on its balance sheet. Let us see how.

Before getting into the details let's get the basic equation here.

Net income = Retained Earnings + Dividends

Alternately,

Retained Earnings/Surplus = Net Income - Dividends

Retained earnings mean all the profits an organization has earned since it came into existence minus dividends.

Now let us see how the retained earnings can be used to decide if a company is inflating its income.

Imagine that I found a company in thee year 2015 and the company had a surplus of $2000 with it at its inception. At the end of the year 2015, my company had a total income of $1500, of which it gave $500 as dividends. It now has $3000 as retained earnings ($1000+$2000).

For the sake of simplicity, suppose that the company had an income of $1,500 every year for three years and the company gave $500 as a dividend every year.

We know that retained earnings correspond to "all the profits since its inception". Let's consider the table below.

Year	Income	Dividend	Expected Cumulative Retained Earning
2015	$1500	$500	$1000+$2000(initial surplus)
2016	$1500	$500	$4000
2017	$1500	$500	$5000

Suppose that you analyzed my company at the end of 2017, that is, over a span of three years and you expect retained earnings to be $5,000.

But imagine that in the annual statement I have shown the retained earnings as $4500. Where did the $500 go?

For example, my company might have had an inventory write-off of $500 in the year 2016. Instead of showing that write-off in P&L and facing a press that reports a fall in earnings, I silently subtracted it from the surplus. No one notices that the surplus decreased. The common things that are hidden using surplus are inventory write-offs, accounts receivables that have gone bad and asset write-offs.

The investors who simply don't bother to check these details will see that my company has high earnings, though actually, its earnings were $500 lesser than reported over a span of three years. They will compare my company with another company in the same industry. They will see that both have a share price of, say, $10. But my company has a high income and thus a low P/E* ratio. Shares of my company look better compared to other companies, though they might be less healthy comparatively. But who cares!!! An intelligent investor should!!!!

It must be reiterated that the examples provided in this chapter are extreme but it is to drive home the point that in day

12 Accounting Discretion Available in Financial Statements

to day affairs of companies, there are many scenarios in which management would be required to use discretion to categorize a spend. For example, say, buying a photocopy machine. Is it capital expenditure, since a new asset is being purchased? Or is it operational expenditure since it is one regular spend to facilitate office work? How about purchasing new pipelines in an existing production plant? Are they maintenance or are they capital expenditure?

Companies do face such dilemmas and they have properly chalked out policies to classify these expenses. But the point of the chapter is to make the readers realize that there are slight differences between the way companies report their finances and at times some companies do inflate their profits by stretching their financial imaginations a bit too far. Nevertheless, such attempts are usually caught by the law and the market sooner or later, but such possibilities do exist and if you are attempting to understand the fundamentals of financial statements, better be aware of them.

*P/E ratio is the price to earnings ratio, which, as the name suggests, provided the ratio between the price of a company and its earnings. If the P/E of a company is low compared to its peers, it indicates that the company shares are a better buy since the price of shares is lower for the same earnings.

13

Cash Management

In the chapter *"Introduction to financial statements"*, we have seen that having the right cash flow is important for companies. This chapter digs a bit deeper into the aspect of cash and explains a bit about the cash conversion cycle.

The cash flow-focused timeline of an enterprise converting raw material into profits is depicted in the following diagram and is explained in subsequent paragraphs.

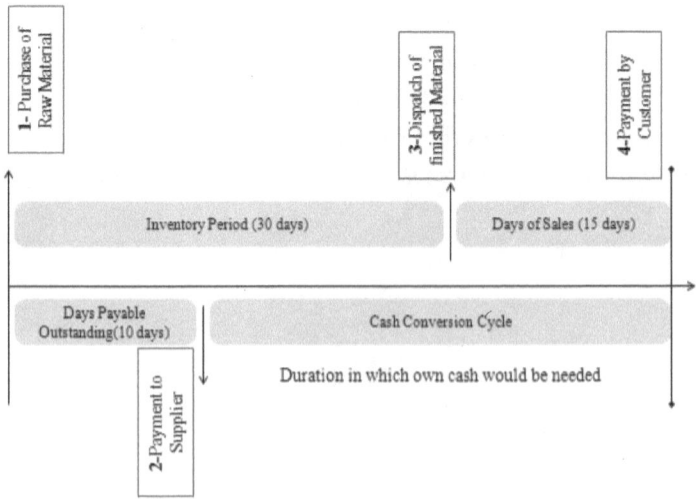

13 Cash Management

For most organizations, the suppliers allow some time before taking the payment for the raw materials and the customers, as well, ask for a certain duration before they could make the payment. This usually happens in any business-to-business sales scenario.

Referring to the diagram, the steps involved are as follows:

1. The organization purchases raw materials and starts converting them into finished products.
2. After a certain duration, say, 10 days, the suppliers of raw material would be required to be paid.
3. The product is sold to the customer.
4. After a certain duration, say, 15 days, the customer makes the payment.

The organization would need cash at step 2 but it won't receive it till step 4. And this needed cash (capital) is borrowed from banks and is called working capital loans. Interest paid by companies on these working capital loans is a huge part of their overall interest expenses. Referring to the diagram, it can be understood that this expense can be reduced if companies:

- Can get better terms from suppliers for a longer duration of paying back (days payable to be increased)
- Can reduce their inventory days
- Can get better terms from customers for a shorter duration of receiving payment

An interesting and extreme example of cash management can be cited from the book 'Factfulness' by Hans Rostling. In one of his assignments Rostling was asked to probe a bid from one of the bidders who was offering to produce medicines at an extremely low price. So, Hans went to the factory to investigate. He asked the company owner how do they make profits while selling their finished good for such a low cost? The response he received is a good lesson about cash management. The company representative responded that his factory has the world's fastest pill-making machine that leverages robotics. Their competitors take significantly more time to produce what they turn around within 4 days. Say, on a Monday, the active ingredient Chloroquine arrives at the factory. By Thursday morning the finished product is at the port. The buyer inspects the pills and signs that he received them, and the money is paid that day into the bank account. The supplier gives them 30 days' credit and customer pays them after only four of those days. That gives them 26 days left to earn interest while the money is sitting in the bank account.[1]

Generally, we don't come across such extreme examples. But the lesson to be picked up here is that if a firm works on reducing its operation cycle time and gets better payment terms, the business saves tons of money on the interest. Let us consider an example. Imagine that your supplier provides you, say, a 0.5% discount if you pay him/her immediately instead of 10 days later. Is it better to take a discount? It depends on how much your bank's rate of interest is. Suppose your bank gives you a working capital loan at a 20% annual interest rate. It means that the interest rate for 10 days would be (20/12)/3 (annual rate divided by 12 months and then one-third of it since 10 days is one-third of a month). This would be 0.55%. So, the bank is giving you a 10-day loan at 0.55%, whereas if you don't take that loan, you are effectively getting a loan at 0.5% from the supplier. Thus, it is better NOT to take that discount and pay after 10 days without a 0.5% discount. Whereas suppose you get a bank loan at 10%, then your bank interest rate for 10 days is 0.27%. Then, go ahead and grab that offer from the supplier. Take a loan from the bank for 10 days and make immediate payment to the supplier. This will make you 0.5%-0.27% better off.

An important corollary that can be devised from the above diagram is inventory management. The lesser the inventory days, the better it is for the company. This can be done by

1. Producing as fast as possible (as was being done in the example provided by Hans Rostling)
2. Avoiding unnecessary inventory, so that products don't sit on the shelves of warehouse/retail outlet for months together before the customer picks it up, or worse, never picks it up.

But too less inventory is also counterproductive for firms. With less than required inventory, a company faces the danger of losing out customers in 'refused sales'. For example, if a customer comes to my warehouse asking for product A, and I convey him/her that I don't have that product with me since I wanted to avoid keeping inventory there are high chances that s/he would go to my competitor for the product rather than waiting for me to produce and provide it. Thus, keeping the right inventory is a science in itself and is one of the most important focus areas in company operations.

Apart from payment management, companies do face a cash crunch in another scenario: if the company is growing at a fast pace.

Let's see the cash constraints that a growing company faces. Imagine that you found a company and you sold products worth $1 million this year and you know that you have a demand of $2 million next year. To cater to that demand, you purchased machines and factory space worth, say, $0.5 million, just to ensure that you are ready for next year's $2 million sales. And also, imagine that you need to pay your day-to-day bills of about $0.8 million this year (raw materials, employee salaries, electricity bills, etc.). Thus, this year, you did a sales of $1 million, made a $0.2 million profit but have an expense of $1.3 million ($0.8 million + $0.5 million). You would need a loan of $0.3 million.

At product level, you are selling profitably, but preparing yourself for future expenses and that is making you take loans. Thus, for a growing company, the cash needs are far more acute since they have to cater to both working capital needs as well as asset building needs. They face a cash crunch since they spend on expansion needs due to heavy growth and constantly miss out on their payment to suppliers, banks, employees and landlords. This makes them vulnerable and the companies die prematurely not due to lack of per product profitability but due to unhealthy cash flow.

14

Financial Ratios – The Tools for Benchmarking Business Performance

Imagine that you own a firm that is spread across 10 countries and has 5 stores in each of those countries. You would find yourself reviewing a performance of 50 outlets. And that translates into tracking fifty instances of parameters, like sales, day-to-day costs, the quantity, value of merchandise and investments.

How would you identify which store of yours is performing best and which aspect of each store needs your attention? Imagine that you start by comparing sales of two stores. But, in many instances, comparing sales might not even make sense. One store might be big and might generate high sales but might have significant running costs associated with it, whereas another store might have very less sales but correspondingly low costs associated with it. The second store seems to be better when compared in terms of profits but the first one makes more sense when compared in terms of sales. The inventory trend of the first one might look high compared to the second one but might be reasonable given its high sales. The high running costs of the first one might look preposterous but they more than make up when you realize that the initial setup cost of the big store was peanuts compared to that of the second small store due to the low local real estate rates of the country.

If you extend this comparison of absolute numbers to fifty other stores, it would be almost impossible to get a sense of what is going on. Thus, comparing the financial performance of entities of different sizes and shapes inevitably has to be done in the form of ratios between a set of parameters. For example, cost to sales, inventory to sales, debt to total worth, etc. And a standardized comparison of these ratios between entities can provide the reviewer a proper sense of which entity is performing better in which aspect. It facilitates benchmarking.

Ratio analysis helps in benchmarking different companies in an industry when ratios are juxtaposed for different firms. It helps in reviewing the financial progress of a single company when its ratios are juxtaposed for different years. For example, if a company has a 'return on capital employed' of 15% and the industry standard is 12%, then it indicates that the company is better than its peers in terms of utilization of capital. The same ratio might be tracked year on year for that company to review whether it is improving or deteriorating in terms of utilization of capital employed.

Management, creditors and investors are the prime users of financial ratios and each one of these users tends to have a slightly different purpose for which they utilize the ratios. For example, short-term and long-term financial creditors are interested in liquidity positions. Long-term financial creditors are interested in long-term debt. Investors are interested in profits since these are highly correlated with a share price. Thus, whether you are a manager of a firm or you are a person who is interested in investing in a firm, understanding the nuances of ratio analysis is indispensable to your survival toolkit.

Since ratio analysis is all about benchmarking, they are usually classified as per the aspect of business execution that they focus on. The following are the important types of ratios:

1. Liquidity ratios – They measure the presence/condition of liquid assets. These ratios primarily cater to short-term creditors.
2. Leverage ratios – They measure the extent of debt and equity. These ratios primarily cater to long-term creditors.
3. Activity ratios – They demonstrate a firm's ability to use assets. These ratios primarily cater to long-term creditors and investors.
4. Profitability ratios – They demonstrate the efficiency of the firm. The primary users of these ratios are management and investors.

Following are the important ratios that might help readers to get a flair for ratio analysis. This is *not* an exhaustive list:

1. Liquidity ratios: As the previous chapter has shown, liquidity is the most important factor for the survival of firms. The following are the important ratios that are used to probe the liquidity-related health of a firm.

1.1. Current Ratio:

$$Current\ Ratio = \frac{Current\ Assets}{Current\ Liabilities}$$

Current ratio provides a hang of the ability of the firm to pay its immediate bills. In other words, would the company still be able to pay its suppliers and immediate lenders if the income of the firm gets disrupted abruptly? If the current ratio is above 1, then chances are high that it would be able to.

But one has to use this ratio with a caveat. The 'composition of current assets' is an important factor to be checked for ascertaining the quality of the current assets. For example, the amount receivable, that is, the expected amount from customers, an element of 'current assets', is expected money and a firm might lose this money if the customer fails to pay dues. Amount receivable is a low-quality current asset compared to, say, cash in hand.

Also, current liabilities don't experience a reduction in their dollar value, whereas current assets sometimes do. For example, inventory may go obsolete and thus useless or debtors may go bankrupt and might turn out to be a bad loan. Thus, it is important to study the composition of current assets along with the raw numbers.

1.2 Quick Ratio:

$$Quick\ Ratio = \frac{Current\ Assets - Inventories}{Current Liabilities}$$

As suggested in the previous section, inventories can go obsolete or might take time to get converted into sales, and thus, the quick ratio is used in tandem with the current ratio for ascertaining liquidity position. A step further to it is the 'cash ratio' mentioned next.

1.3 Cash Ratio:

$$Cash Ratio = \frac{Cash + Marketable\ Securities}{Current Liabilities}$$

14 Financial Ratios – The Tools for Benchmarking Business Performance

2. **Leverage Ratio:** As mentioned earlier, these ratios are meant to cross-check if the firm has taken too much debt.

2.1. Debt Ratio:

$$Debt\ Ratio = \frac{Total\ Debt}{Total\ Debt + Net\ Worth}$$

The net worth in the above ratio comes with its own caveats. It shouldn't have too much of intangible elements like goodwill or, say, patents. Also, if the net worth has increased significantly due to the recent increase in inventory without a corresponding rise in sales that too would be a point of concern.

2.2. Debt to Equity Ratio:

$$Debt\ to\ Equity\ Ratio = \frac{Total\ Debt}{Net\ Worth}$$

3. **Activity Ratio:** The ratios under this group help the reviewer understand the performance of firms in terms of utilization of means of production. Provided below are two important activity ratios:

3.1. Inventory Turnover ratio:

$$Inventory\ Turnover\ Ratio = \frac{Cost\ of\ Goods\ Sold}{Average\ Inventory}$$

This ratio measures the performance within a duration, usually the financial year.

Consider a retailer who purchases $1000 worth of shoes every month and sells merchandise that costs him/her $800 every month (this is not the price of goods sold, it is the cost of the goods sold. The retailer would obviously mark up the price for his/her margin when deciding the price of goods sold).

Inventory at beginning of period = $0
Inventory at end of 12 months = ($1000−$800)*12 = $2400
Average inventory = ($0+$2400)/2 = $1200
Cost of goods sold (COGS) = $800*12 = $9600

Number of times retailer was able to completely deplete the inventory = COGS/Average inventory = $9600/$1200 = 8

Imagine if the same retailer sold monthly merchandise costing $500.

Inventory at beginning of period = $0
Inventory at end of 12 months = ($1000 −$500)*12 = $6000
Average inventory = ($0+ $6000)/2 = $3000
COGS = $500*12 = $6000
New inventory turnover ratio = $6000/$3000 = 2

In the first case, the retailer was able to move the whole inventory of shoes that s/he had for 8 times, which means that the sales are going reasonably fast. Whereas, in the second case, the retailer was able to turn his/her inventory only twice. The sales are going pretty slow. A lot of shoes are sitting in his/her shop and not getting converted into money. Stuff is piling up in the store. In the second case, the retailer should look at where is s/he going wrong. Either s/he is purchasing too much stock and no customer is coming to buy the stock or sh/e is purchasing the wrong stock and customers are coming but are not finding the kind of shoes they want. So, s/he should, based on diagnosis, either purchase the right inventory or the right amount of inventory (reduce the $1000 purchase to, say, $600), so that his/her money doesn't remain stuck on the shelves in the form of shoes and s/he uses that money to pay her bills and debts. Firms should align their inventory strategy with their overall operations strategy and marketing strategy. If a firm is, say, a trader in luxury merchandise and it operates by providing a high variety to customers, then they would be required to keep a lot of inventory. The high amount of inventory, and thus, low turns, would be compensated by the high margins they can charge on those luxury goods. On the other hand, if they operate in no-fringe merchandise, where customers come for a better price of regular products and not variety, then high focus on the right inventory would be essential for such a firm.

3.2. Asset Turnover ratio:

$$Asset\ turnover\ ratio = \frac{Net\ sales}{Average\ of\ total\ Assets}$$

This ratio provides an insight into how effectively are assets being deployed. A few pointers about asset turnover ratio (ATR) are as follows:

- Other things being equal, the higher the ATR, the better the performance of the firm.
- Usually, ATR is higher in low-margin industries. For example, a newspaper delivery person might have only a bicycle as his/her assets. And his/her ATR might be very high compared to, say, a retailer whose asset is a big outlet. But given that s/he earns very less margin on the business, ATR isn't a good indicator to compare the newspaper delivery person with the retailer. Thus, ATR shouldn't be used in isolation for comparing two different industries.

- A low ATR might mean one or more of the following problems:
  - *Low sales compared to available capacity.* Imagine there are two retailers with similar-sized stores. One is using his/her outlet very effectively while the second one is not using it to make enough sales. ATR of the second one would be low due to the under-utilization of capacity. Either s/he should trim down his/her capacity or should increase the sales.
  - *Too much inventory compared to sales.* Inventory is accounted for as an asset. Considering the example of the shoe retailer, mentioned in previous paragraphs, the retailer had too much inventory compared to sales and it would be reflected in his/her low ATR.

Return on assets is a close cousin of ATR in terms of the financial assessment. Here, the number that is compared against the total asset is 'profit' rather than revenue. In terms of classification, it is supposed to be in the next section since it is a profitability ratio.

4. Profitability Ratios:

4.1. Profit Margin: It is the ratio between profit and revenue. Profit is assessed at three levels– gross profit, operating profit and net profit. Gross profit is measured by comparing variable costs with revenue. Operating profit is measured by comparing direct running costs with revenue whereas net profit is calculated by comparing revenue with all the costs (including the annual component of capital expense, that is, depreciation, interest expenses, taxes, etc.).

5. DuPont Analysis:

Let's end this chapter with a very robust framework that captures end to end performance of a firm in a single equation.

The analysis has been popularized by DuPont Corporation. The framework is depicted in the equation below:

$$Return\ on\ Equity = \frac{Profit}{Equity} = \frac{Profit}{Revenue} * \frac{Revenue}{Total\ Assets} * \frac{Total\ Assets}{Equity}$$

$$= Profit\ Margin * ATR * Equity\ Mulitiplier$$

The higher the first two elements in the above equation, the better is the company's performance, whereas it is the other way round for the third component, which, if too high, indicates that there is very less equity in the firm and assets are being funded by taking a lot of debt. The equation brilliantly captures the idea that return on equity, that is, the return on money shareholders put into a firm, is based on profitability, the efficient utilization of assets and the use of the right amount of debt.

This chapter has covered a few most utilized ratios but the list is not exhaustive. Many ratios are applicable to specific industries and situations but have been omitted here. The primary purpose of the chapter is to drive the point home that ratios are an important instrument of business performance review. They demand some amount of practice and keen-eyed focus to master, but this effort is worth it because of the insights they provide about performance and investing.

15

Cost at Which Companies Obtain Money

Anything that has a utility and is not one of nature's free gifts has to be paid for to be obtained. Money is no different. Since money is something that is scarce and is not easily available, you obtain it by paying a cost on it. This cost is called interest.

Imagine you need $10,000, say, for financing your education, and your brother has promised you $5000. He asked you to return this $5000 next year. You approached a bank for the remaining amount and they issued you the money and asked you to pay $5500 at the end of the year.

So what is the cost at which you obtained $5000 from your brother? It was $0. What was the cost at which you obtained $5000 from the bank? It was $500 for $5000, that is, 10% cost. What is the cost of the total money you obtained? It is $500/$10000, that is, 5%. The same can be calculated using the equation below.

$$Average\ cost\ of\ money = \frac{0\% * 5000 + 10\% * 5000}{10000} = 5\%$$

Let's make it a bit more complicated. Now imagine that your brother had only $2000 and you obtained the remaining $3000 through a government-supported scheme for students

15 Cost at Which Companies Obtain Money

in which they provide up to $3000 to students for $150 cost. In percentage terms, the cost of $3000 is 150/3000, that is, 5%. So, what is now the cost of the total money you got? Your total cost is $650 ($500 for the bank and $150 for the government scheme) for arranging $10,000. In percentage terms, it is 650/10000, that is, 6.5%. The same can be calculated as follows:

$$Cost\ of\ money = \frac{0\% * 2000 + 5\% * 3000 + 10\% * 5000}{10000} = 6.5\%$$

You can see that your total cost of fees (let's call it capital) is based on interest rate in proportion to weightage of each chunk of money that you got from different sources. Thus, the above cost is called the "weighted average cost of capital" (WACC). It can be complicated further by having a few more sources over multiple years, but the idea remains the same.

The struggle of companies to get money is not much different from a student struggling to get money. Companies, too, need a lot of money to run their day-to-day affairs. This money is called "capital" and the cost at which they obtain money from different sources is called WACC.

Companies usually have two sources of money:

i. Money that has been put in by share holders: This is called equity. Share holders get a chunk of profit proportionate to the number of shares they own. This chunk of profit that the company gives to shareholders, in the form of dividends, is the "cost" of this capital.
ii. Money borrowed from banks: This is called debt. Companies pay interest on this loan amount. This interest is the "cost" of this portion of the capital.

The final cost of capital of any company is the weighted average of these two sources of money – the WACC!

A few pointers around the cost of capital:

The cost of debt is usually less compared to the cost of equity. The reason being that debt has security associated with it. Companies repay their loans before calculating profits. This higher assurance of being paid loan means it is less risky for banks compared to the risk that share holders have since shareholders get money only when all expenses are catered to and there is still some profit remaining. This lower risk, in turn, means that banks are willing to charge lesser cost (interest rate) compared to the percentage of profit (in the form of dividends) that shareholders expect.

A corollary of this element of "risk" is the fact that banks give away loans to some companies for cheap compared to others. If a company is big, has less overall debt and is making a stable profit for many years then, there are high chances that it would be paying back in the future without facing much trouble. Thus, banks charge, say, 2% less interest rate from a well-established company compared to a start-up whose business abilities are yet to be proven. There is a whole lot of literature around this relationship between risk and expected returns/interest rates. One can read about CAPM to get an in-depth (pun intended) understanding of the risk-return relationship for capital funding.

If the cost of debt is usually less than equity, then why don't companies take only debt and no equity for funding their capital needs? If there is too much debt, then the company faces the "risk" of defaulting, which, in turn, would make the banks charge a higher percentage on their loans. Thus, the right trade-off between debt and equity is a constant tussle, which the CFOs face to ensure getting capital at the cheapest cost.

16

Company Valuations – Simplified

Every now and then, we come across news that reads something like "So and so company valued at $15 billion", or, say, "Company X's valuation went up seven times in last year".

This article is an attempt to explain how the valuations of the companies work. What it is with the rise and fall in the value of those privately and publicly held companies?

The methods followed to value a company are not much different from the methods you use to value other assets. Just imagine that you have an advertising hoarding panel on the terrace of your apartment that you want to sell to someone. For how much will you sell the hoarding?

Techniques of Valuation:

You will value a company by three methods:

1. You will measure that if some person puts an advertisement on that space, he will get an annual rent of, say, $10,000. And you expect that this rent will continue for the next five years. So, you will sell the hoarding at $50,000 (5*10000). In short, you have "valued" your hoarding at $50000.

2. Or you will see for how much the hoardings in the apartments in the vicinity are being sold. And you will put the price of your hoarding the same as that of the comparable hoardings.
3. Or you will estimate how much money you have put to make the hoarding panel, the wood and steel that went into it. And that will be the value of your advertising panel.

By the way, the first method that uses the estimation of income is called intrinsic valuation, the second method is called relative valuation and the third method is called contingent claim valuation.

As you might understand, the first method that is "intrinsic valuation" is the most commonly used method of valuating a company. So, if you estimate that company X will get a cash flow of $1 billion every year and it will remain in business for the next 15 years, you value it at approximately $15 billion ($1 billion *15). The trick behind the whole valuation lies in estimating these two elements: estimated annual cash flows and expected life of a company. There is one more element in valuation that complicates it slightly – "Time value of money."

The CAPM:

What exactly is the time value of money? Imagine that someone gives you an offer whether you would like $1000 now or you want it a year later. Obviously, you will prefer it now, because you know that after a year, the purchasing power of $1000 will reduce due to inflation. This preference for present money and the expectation that its value will reduce over time is called the "time value of money". Suppose you imagine that there will be annual inflation of 5% (that is, the purchasing power of $1000 will reduce by 5% over one year) then you will value it at 1000/1.05 = $952). If you see that there is higher market volatility and the inflation will be, say, 10%, then your "after one year $1000" will be worth only $909 (1000/1.1) to you. Thus, higher the risk, higher will be the discount rate "r" and the lower will be your current value of a future cash flow.

Net Present Value = Cash flow/(1+r) + Cash flow/(1+r)^2 + Cash flow/(1+r)^3.......

Imagine that you consider the company that you are valuing to be very risky. Then, you will make "r" in the above equation very high. Thus, the risky company will be valued lesser. This "r" is called WACC that we discussed in the previous chapter.

The problem of predicting the exact value:

Now that you have understood that every valuation is about three simple numbers: cash flows, r value and the duration for which the company will remain in business, you can easily become an investment banker. The only problem is that these three simple numbers are not easy to be calculated accurately. Just imagine that twenty years back, you were valuing a firm that is into trading photography films. You were happy that the firm will get a lot more sales since "instant photography", a technology in which you click a picture and get a printout from the camera right then and there, would be the next big thing. You estimated that it will survive for the next ten years and will generate annual revenue of about $500 million. (You valued it at approx. $5 billion (500*10)). But there was just one problem: It was digital photography that became popular. Instant photography cameras just were not being sold and the trading firm that you loved so much went into loss. In short, due to market disruption, the value of the company fell drastically. The shares that were priced at, say, $100 in 2000 would now be a fraction of that amount.

Such disruptions and valuation changes keep happening in almost every industry. A competitor has strongly entered the market and is taking its market share – The firm that had $100/share suddenly falls to $80/share. These changes in valuations, in general, are called "market correction".

The sentiment effect on Market Corrections: In the case of publicly held companies, these "corrections", at times, go overboard and panic grips the shareholders though there is no big threat to future cash flows to the company. You can't help it: when Washington sneezes, Wall Street catches fever!

So, by now, you might have understood, that if a company is valued at $1 billion, it doesn't mean that it has $1 billion in its bank account or has machinery/land worth $1 billion. Rather, it is just a notional number for equity holders to value their investment. For example, if an investor has estimated a company to be worth of $100 million, s/he may invest $10 million and take a 10% stake.

So, whether you are a venture capitalist, an angel investor or a hedge fund manager. The secret to your success is predicting the future as accurately as possible about the abilities of the companies to survive and generate cash flow. The better you predict, the more accurate valuation you will do and the more successful will you be as an investor.

Premium paid for purchasing complete firm:

Often, we come across a piece of news that says that company X has acquired company Y, whose market price is $10/share for a price of $12/share. Why do acquiring firms pay this premium (in this case, 20%)? When we go to buy a dress, we don't tell the shopkeeper, "Here… keep $20, though you are selling it for $15 to everyone!"

16 Company Valuations – Simplified

That extra premium is for the fact that company X is acquiring the "control" of the target "Y" along with the assets. The market price of $10/share was for assets. The extra $2/share is being paid for the control... a control that can ensure higher returns if the $10 assets are better utilized. How do we evaluate whether this $2/share is the right value of control.

To begin with, let us try to understand what is market capitalization? The market capitalization of a firm, in long run, reflects the best estimation of all the expected future cash flows from an asset.

Imagine a company that has a life of one year and is expecting a $100 profit (cash flow to be precise) at the end of the year. The value of that company would be $100. But, there is a small catch, the value of $100 at year-end would be slightly less than $100 at hand (prices keep rising and $100 doesn't get us the same stuff next year). Thus, the precise value of the company would be:

$100/(1+expected rate of return or cost of financing)

Instead of $100, if "C" is the cash flow expected and it is for two years instead of one, then the value of the company would be [C/(1+r) + C/(1+r)^2]. After 3 years, it is [C/(1+r) + C/(1+r)^2 + C/1(1+r)^3] and so on and so forth. Here, "r" is the expected rate of return or cost of financing the firm.

Instead of going into the precise math, it can be understood from the above equation that the value of a company can be increased by the following means:[1]

1. Increasing the value of C every year
2. Increasing the number of years for which "C" is getting generated
3. Decreasing the value of "r" (since r is in the denominator)

And acquiring companies hope to do the above three things by exercising the control that they acquire by paying the premium. What is the practical way of getting the above three things done?

Increasing the value of "C" (cash flow):

1. Increasing cash flow from existing assets is done by
   (a) Asset redeployment: Using an asset for a purpose that generates more cash flow. Example: Converting a warehouse space in a market area into a retail outlet so that it generates revenue
   (b) Improved operating efficiency: Example: Lesser staff per retail outlet, so that costs associated come down and thus the firm gets better cash flow.
   (c) Identifying where the tax burden can be eliminated in a legal and legitimate way
   (d) Reducing capital investment and working capital needs: Example: Having the right inventory at outlets, so that lesser money is stuck in form of merchandise and thus lesser money is needed to be borrowed to run the company.
2. Increasing cash flow from new assets: Example: Creating new retail outlets that give high business compared to older outlets using cash that was lying unutilized in company's bank account

Increasing the number of years during which C (or growth in C) is getting generated:

1. By creating a reasonable competitive advantage by say innovation or better brand building.

Decreasing the value of r:

1. By changing the financing mix: "r", the average of the cost at which the firm is getting loans and getting equity, needs to be at an optimum level. Usually, the cost at which the loan is issued is lesser than the cost at which the equity is issued. But, too much loan reduces the ability of a firm to pay back and thus the banks/lenders start expecting higher interest rates when there is too much loan on a company. Thus, the cost of financing the firm increases. On the other hand, equity brings a sense of stability to the firm, but it is costly and thus shouldn't be the only means of funding a firm. Thus, the right balance between equity and debt reduces the cost of financing a firm. Some targets have an opportunity hidden in this mix.

If an acquirer sees an opportunity in any of the above three options in target, then it can pay a premium over the existing cost, because it can hope to recover the premium by mending the ways of the target once it is under its control. Thus paying some premium is justified while purchasing good asset which is being badly run, since a well-run target would already have its parameters at an optimum level and thus not much can be extracted by a mere change of control.

17

Investing in Stocks

This chapter is meant to explain the logic behind stock pricing (though this logic usually gets washed away during stock market euphoria and distress).

Let us begin by understanding the theoretical underpinnings of how the stock price of a company is arrived at. Imagine that you started a company that is supposed to exist only for one year and it is expected to earn a 'profit' of $1000 at the end of the year. You need initial money to run the firm. You approach nine of your friends and request each of them to contribute equally so that each one of you gets a 10% 'share' of the company. How much would each of you consider appropriate to invest to get the 10% of profit, that is, $100 at end of the year? Obviously, it would be lesser than $100… may be an investment of about $90. Now, let us complicate things a bit. If the company is going to stay for 5 years instead of one year how much would each one of you consider appropriate to invest? The expected income or profit from the venture is going to be 5*$1000, that is, $5000. So, each one of you would believe that an investment (is it the share price?) of *less than* $500 would make sense since you expect to get $100 each year for the next 5 years.

This ratio between the price of the share (in the vicinity of $500 in this case) and earning or income or profit, that is,

17 Investing in Stocks

'price-to-earning ratio' (p/e ratio) is an important ratio that is considered in stock trading.

The manner in which you arrived at $100 or $500 price in case of your venture is technically the same in which stock prices are arrived at for a multi-billion company trading on the stock exchange. The ownership in the case of mega-firms is not in terms of percentages but in terms of the number of units of shares, since it is not 10 persons among whom the company is divided, it is in order of hundreds of thousands.

As seen above, this stock price factors in two things:

- The expected annual income of the venture.
- The number of years the venture is expected to exist at the above income levels.

The key word in the above two factors is 'expected'. There is an element of uncertainty in both the annual income of the venture and the number of years it is going to survive. You never know how long and to what extent is the company going to enjoy the customers' patronage and survive competitors' onslaught.

Say, for example, you know that in the above-mentioned firm, annual income is going to be $3000 from the third year on. Then, you would calculate that 2*$1000+3*$3000, that is, $11,000 is the expected return from the venture and thus you would assume that a share price of less than $1,100 (10% of 11,000) is a reasonable investment. The current p/e ratio of 5 of the above venture and the share price of $500 seems a great catch to you. You might, in fact, reach one of your partner friends and try to buy their 10% share. The price of your share, in this case, is $500, whereas its actual 'value' is in the vicinity of $1100. The one who develops this knack of finding the ventures whose share 'price' is significantly less than their 'value' is the one who tends to become a successful investor. When all your friends find your hidden secret of 'factoring future income', then each one of them would be ready to pay $1100 for the share. The share price of the venture would, within no time, reach $1100 and the p/e to 11 (1100/$100).

As seen in the above case, the share price keeps gyrating in face of any new update related to the company. It can be due to company-based developments, like the introduction of new products, entry into new markets or, say, signing of a new pact with a competitor. And more often than not, it is not so related factors, like macroeconomic interest rates, industry trends, commodity prices, presidential elections, etc. that fluctuate the prices (in both positive and negative directions) beyond the reasonable range. Oh!! the raw material price has reduced; the income is going to increase for the company so I am happy paying $520 for each share rather than $500. Oh!! People are traveling to Dubai this holiday season!! The company is going to have fewer sales in USA; I am going to pay only $480 for its share. These changes, more often than not, swing prices far more than needed (Though nobody with their entire wisdom can precisely predict this 'needed' swing). Also, the market price changes are reported and discussed so much that they tend to take a rhythm and momentum of their own, independent of how realistically are they related to the company's fundamentals.

The market fluctuations when they make prices swoop too low are the most important opportunities for those who are considering investing in stock trading. So, a reasonably good *initial* step for identifying the right opportunities in stock trading is looking for companies with a low price-to-earnings

17 Investing in Stocks

ratio. These can provide you with candidate stocks that you can probe further. A firm with a p/e of 5 has probably a better chance of upside than the one that is already at a p/e of 11 since the one at 11 has already factored in a higher future uncertain income compared to the one at 5. Such candidate stocks with a low p/e are found mostly during the time when the stock market has recently undergone a 'correction', a euphemistic word for the market crash.

Though there is no sure way of becoming a legendary investor, the following set of steps can provide better odds of success:

- In stock trading, invest only the amount that you can afford to park without impacting your consumption levels. It is the amount that you would not need in, say, the next three years in desperation. Because if you sell in desperation, you would sell your stocks at whatever price available and usually that would be a very low price.
- The firms with a low price compared to earnings (Low p/e ratio) are a good starting point.
- Study the companies that you picked for their fundamentals and financial ratios. You can use this book for doing that or use the outstanding books mentioned at end of this book.
- Check if the company has good fundamentals through the following factors:
  - If it is a well-established firm,
    - Then, check for consistent income for the previous 5 odd years. The income shouldn't fluctuate too much year on year.
    - Ensure that there is no sharp rise in debt compared to the rise in income.

- o If it is a not much-known firm, check if there is a potential for income growth. You would be required to know the industry in which the firm is operating and should test the potential of the firm through feelers like how excited are its customers online and offline. How long is the line on its cash counters, etc.
- o All the above steps are meant to ensure that the value you arrive at for the share of a company is higher than the price that it is being traded at. If you purchase a very good stock at a wrong price, then you are not going to make many profits through share trading.
- Hold the company long enough till the market realizes the potential of the stock in terms of its earnings and starts buying it (In our imaginary company, the rate is increasing from $500 to $1100 when your friends realized the true potential).

Following this disciplined approach of valuing a company and holding it long enough for the price to reach its true value is better than purchasing stocks randomly on unsolicited tips and expecting that someone else is going to pay more for the same stock in the future.

In contrast with the above algorithmic approach, many individuals putting money in stocks just look at share price gyrations and join the dance. And such gyrations might provide you a quick buck as part of beginner's luck, but they are dangerous in the long run. When price fluctuations are getting affected more due to macro factors, like, say, the rate of interest of banks or change of governments, than the inherent value of the business, then they tend to fluctuate unpredictably and chances of losing money would be as high as the irrationality driving the prices around.

18

Costing

Arriving at cost of a product or a service is challenging for organizations. But they are required to find these costs because costs guide their selling price and the right selling price ensures the right profitability.

But why is arriving at the right costs challenging for organizations? Let's understand the intricacies of costing using an example.

Imagine that there is a firm that manufactures two products – product A and product B. Product A happens to be a regular product that is, say, sold at $250, whereas product B is a special product for which customers pay a premium and it is sold at $300.

The costs associated with these two products can be divided into two categories:

1. Direct Costs: For example, raw material costs, specific packaging material costs and labor costs for the personnel who are directly and only involved in the production of the specific products.
2. Indirect Costs: For example, the electricity that is used across the factory, procurement personnel who work to procure supplies for both the products and marketing personnel who work for promoting both the products.

Part – II: Business Management, Finance and Company Operations

Let us consider that the products have the costs as provided in Table 1. For the sake of simplicity, let us consider that the indirect costs mentioned in the table are the salaries of three procurement personnel and three marketing personnel, who are working for both the products and the company is paying $10,000 to each of them.

The company attributes costs to each of its products as listed in Table 1. The indirect cost of $60,000 is divided between the two products in the ratio of the quantity of each product manufactured.

Table 1						
Product	Qty	Material Cost/piece	Indirect Cost	Indirect Cost Attributable	Indirect Cost/Piece	Total Cost
A (regular)	500	$120	$60,000	$60,000 x 500/600 = $50,000	50,000/500 = $100	$220
B (special)	100	$150		$60,000 x 100/600 = $10,000	$10,000/100 = $100	$250

As per the above table, since the quantity of product A is five times that of product B, the indirect cost associated with product A is $50,000 whereas that with product B is $10,000.

The profits from each product based on Table 1 would be as follows:

Table 2			
Product	Selling Price	Cost	Profit Margin/Piece
A	$250	$220	$30
B	$300	$250	$50

18 Costing

The indirect cost attributed to the ratio of the quantity of production is a simple way of dividing the costs between multiple products. But is it the right way? To answer the question, let us again consider the two products A & B of the above-mentioned organization. To precisely calculate the indirect costs, the deployment of the six personnel needs to be probed further.

Let us consider the following scenario. Since product B is a special product, two persons out of the three procurement employees focus on procuring raw materials related to B. Also, the customers choosing product B need special attention and two persons working full time from the marketing department cater to product B. In such a scenario, the costs associated with the two products might look a bit different as depicted in Table 3.

Table 3						
Product	Qty	Material Cost/piece	Indirect Cost	Indirect Cost Attributable	Indirect Cost/Piece	Total Cost
A (regular)	500	$120	$60,000	$30,000 x 1/3 +$30,000x1/3	20,000/500 = $40	$160
B (special)	100	$150		$30,000 x 2/3+ $30,000 x 2/3	$40,000/100 = $400	$550

$2/3^{rd}$ portion of the $30,000 salaries of both procurement and marketing departments are to be attributed to product B since two persons out of three in both the departments cater to the product. In such a scenario, what would the profit margins look like for the two products?

Table 4			
Product	Selling Price	Cost	Profit Margin/Piece
A	$250	$160	$90
B	$300	$550	-$250

The management that is focusing on product B, imagining that it is more profitable (as depicted in Table 2), would be completely wrong since, in reality, product B is a loss-making product if considered from the point of view of resource utilization and activities done on it. Thus, dividing the costs in the ratio of the quantity of production in a multi-product scenario is not correct if the resource utilization among the products is non-uniform.

The second method of costing as depicted in Tables 3 and 4 is called activity-based costing. It was proposed by Robin Cooper and Robert Kaplan in their classic HBR article titled 'Measuring Cost Right'. It has its limitations. A lot of work-study and employee surveying would be needed to conclude that two people out of three work only for product B, or 65% of factory electricity is used for product X or 30% of the supervisor's time goes into solving problems arising due to product Z. But, if done economically and with reasonable accuracy, such a cost attribution helps organizations a lot in terms of getting their priorities right.

19

A Few Pointers for Start Ups

This write up is a collection of pointers from different sources to help anyone who is considering starting a company on his/her own:

Brainstorm the following:

Irrespective of the business you want to take a plunge into, chalk out the following basics:

During Idea Phase:

1. *Your Value Proposition*: What is the one thing that you will deliver to the customer (Example: An online retailer's value proposition is providing products cheaply at the doorstep of customers from distant vendors). The value proposition should be checked on:
   1. Are there any substitute products that serve the same purpose for your customers as your value proposition?
   2. Quality of idea/product: If something is plain and obvious, it cannot become a great story by beating the trumpet of advertising. Salesmen need a good product to make good sales.

3. Uniqueness: If your design/idea/product is good, but it is so straightforward that anyone can imitate it, then you cannot get ahead of the race.

2. *Who is your customer*: In terms of age, demographics, preferences, purchasing habits and purchasing ability.
3. The *cost* at which you will be able to generate that value proposition
4. *Willingness of the customer to pay*: We tend to be so much in awe of our bright new idea that we tend to believe that customers will flock to our product once it is in the market. There is a word for this feeling - "pro-innovation bias". Be aware of it. Find out whether customers are willing to pay the price at which you are offering them product profitably. Surveys don't help here. Create a minimum viable product in the cheapest possible way and reach out to the early adopters who are willing to experiment. Observe their response in their natural habitat.
5. How and at what price are your competitors producing the product?
6. *Necessary Ecosystem*: You can run an e-commerce website because you have an internet that can easily transfer images across, ensure a safe transaction of money and is easily accessible from everywhere. Imagine an e-commerce company being formed in 1990 (the year when the internet took shape), it might have died because of too slow transfer of images or due to lack of safe methods of e-transactions. So, if you find an idea that is brilliant, has a great team and is cheap but is way too ahead of its time, just don't invest in it. You cannot run a fast car on a mud road.

7. *Political, Cultural and Economic Factors:* If you want to sell cars worth $100000 in, say, Afghanistan, you won't find buyers. Your idea will die. You need to go to Dubai to sell it. Big ships are launched only in deep water.

During Initial Growth Phase

1. *Minimum Viable Product (MVP)*: Don't wait till you make a 100% complete product. You would be required to make a lot of course corrections based on customer feedback. So, brainstorm about an MVP that satisfies the basic needs of customers and market it immediately.
2. *Get market product fit*: A good product will survive only if it is marketed in the appropriate market to appropriate customers.
3. *Scalability*: How do you plan to grow, how much do you plan to grow and at what rate do you plan to grow.
4. *Cash Flow*: When starting a company, ensure that you have enough cash for running it at least for a year and a half without relying on the revenues of your end product. At the start, you would need a lot of money to create your assets (say, factory or initial prototype). Be prudent and never spend on plush furniture and costly real estate. There is a reason why most of the big companies started in dorm rooms and garages. The ones that started in plush offices probably crumbled under the weight of their real estate rents!
5. *Good team*: Execution is as important as the idea. You cannot run a brilliant idea with a team that is not dedicated and lacks the necessary skills. Hence, if you are thinking of investing in some project that has a shabby team but has a good idea, think twice. It may not grow into a great story.

Long-term Sustenance:

1. *The Hedgehog Concept*: I am borrowing this from Good to Great by Jim Collins. Darwin and natural selection, Marx and class struggle, Freud and sub-conscious. They used their one single theory to explain every aspect of our life: Why we buy and sell, why we fall in love, why we work, why we do what we do. In a similar way, your company should have one concept around which it should be able to do everything. That metric may be profit per ton of finished product (if you are a manufacturer), profit per square yard of space (if you own a showroom), profit per employee (if you are in the service industry), etc. There can be a hundred metrics of measuring your company's success, you need to find the one that is most appropriate and completely aligned with the value proposition of your firm.

2. Irrespective of how rational or irrational your brainstorming is, the results of your endeavor will remain uncertain both in negative and positive directions. Your execution, luck, the condition of your industry, the condition of the overall economy… there are many things beyond your control that control you. So, don't think too much. Start the act… but keep the safeguards in place.

A few nuggets of wisdom from " The Lean Startup" by Eric Ries:

- Have your value hypothesis (what do you think is the value your start-up is adding) and growth hypothesis (how big do you think your firm will grow) and test those hypotheses by whatever means you can.

19 A Few Pointers for Start Ups

- Constantly learn as you work. So, keep deciding in between proceeding and pivoting. Proceeding is doing what you are doing and pivoting is a course correction, taking insights from the market.
- Use Pareto analysis... which 20% of features give 80% of value to your product or service. Start with those features rather than a complete product.
- Surveys usually don't work... when you ask someone would you purchase this, they tend to, say, yes and immediately if you ask them "ok purchase this then", they will, for sure, smirk. So, the best way is to start cheap, sell it, learn from your sales and change your product if the market asks you to.

The image of an entrepreneur is that of a young (usually) man in his twenties catching a flight to present his next big food delivery idea to venture capitalists.

The stories about business ideas on napkins, first products in garages, rag to riches anecdotes and dorm rooms to boardrooms narrations have romanticized entrepreneurship into a glamorized form. This form resembles entrepreneurship as much as a scaled-down model in an architect's lobby resembles the actual sky scrapper that is being built. It has a lot more to it than developing an app or pitching to venture capitalists. Entrepreneurship is about creating a beautiful picture from the palette of opportunity, technology, effort and foresight. Uncertainty is the middle name of entrepreneurship.

And it is not always about a multi-billion valuation or turnover. Running a business that ensures satisfying a niche market with special needs is as much entrepreneurial as is creating a multi-national firm. Also, it is not always about new technology being converted into a business. Richard

Branson, the billionaire who found Virgin Empire, or Sam Walton of Walmart didn't deploy radically new technologies to create businesses. But they are among the most successful entrepreneurs this planet has ever produced.

What are the most necessary traits to be an entrepreneur? Maybe the following:

Foresight:

Consider Bill Gates. He came of age at a time when hardware was the focus of the IT industry. The conventional wisdom of the era was that people buy computers and then write their own programs to use them, the way people buy a car and drive them around themselves. But Bill Gates foresaw that making software will be far more challenging than moving around a car and would need specialization. He saw the market opportunity in selling software when the whole world was focused on selling hardware. May it be Dr. Anji Reddy who foresaw that India can be a supplier of pharmaceutical products to the USA due to regulatory changes of 1984 or may it be Phil Knight who foresaw that Americans need cheap and good quality shoes. Entrepreneurs have the ability to see opportunities on the horizon much before others.

So, if you want to be a successful entrepreneur, develop acumen in a single field and start identifying opportunities in that field. It can be either artificial intelligence or it can be a construction business… it doesn't matter but be the one who grasped the idea first if you want to make it big.

Ability to identify gaps:

People come together in complex and at times innovative ways to carry out economic activity. Say, for example, a brand owner doesn't have all the money needed to run a hundred stores, he would partner with others and provide them the merchandise. The partners, in turn, would take responsibility for running the stores and take loans to get outlet space. This is called a franchise system. In this case, both the brand owner and the franchise store owners happen to be entrepreneurs. They probe and, based on market feelers, take the risk of putting up money and effort to fulfill a gap. Identification of the right gap with an ability to fulfill it profitably is what separates a good entrepreneur from a bad one.

Extreme endurance:

Entrepreneurship and its challenges drain you of your cash and your emotional reserve. Spending a million to buy a warehouse, when your annual revenue is half that amount, you need a big faith in the future and nerves to endure the failures that come while taking such decisions. If you are a kind who needs a peptalk whenever your favorite team lost a match, then you are not the entrepreneurial type. They are the ones who give pep talks and see the silver lining even in the darkest clouds.

Ability to develop a team:

Irrespective of how intelligent or hardworking you are, you cannot be an entrepreneur on your own. Entrepreneurship needs an individual who can gather a group. Even the firms that got famous for a single individual had a set of mandarins behind the star CEO. Thus, to be an entrepreneur you need the ability to identify people-job fit as well as have a personality trustworthy enough so that people make your dream their own.

Ability to convince (the supplier/the customer/the investor/the spouse/the family):

An entrepreneur is a person with a "never say die" attitude. They need high reserves of whatever it takes to convince people. The suppliers will be demanding their money when it is needed to be spent on expanding business, the investors would be wary about future prospects of the business whenever you go to them for the next release of funds and the family would be worried about you leaving a steady job to take up a roller coaster ride. You need to convince each one of them that it is going to be okay.

Some connections:

Though it is usually not mentioned, the ease with which you can win over investors and suppliers, if not customers, depends a lot on who you are as well. If you have connections in silicon valley or are from an Ivy League /IIT/IIM, your odds of getting funding do increase multi-fold. Though capitalism is said to be the first cousin of meritocracy, the who and who do get a head start when it comes to starting a business even if they don't get a head start while running a business.

Conclusion

To condense the book in a few words, it can be said that it is an attempt to clarify the science of transactions. An economic transaction takes place only when the parties involved agree on a price and disagree on value. For example, if I am selling a bag to a person for $10, its value is less than $10 for me and is more than $10 for the person purchasing it. This simple idea is the reason for every purchase or sale people make, whether a commodity or luxury, whether a perishable or an edifice, whether a factory or a pin being made in that factory. And this book has attempted to better understand the whole structure that is standing on this simple idea.

This structure has grown big due to the human tendency of performing transactions, creating, and storing wealth. Catalyzed by human ingenuity to create newer means of producing and consuming goods and performing services, economic transactions have led to the creation of business empires, megacities and humming bazaars. The impact of ideologies, geographies and natural resources has complicated the functioning of the economic and transactional structure further.

Studying this structure is multi-dimensional by its very nature. Since money is all about numbers, economics is a cousin of basic mathematics. But, at times, it involves the study of how people behave, so psychology is always around the corner on the path of economic study. In a few other scenarios, it is all about geography. Sometimes, the social norms and regulations decide how much wealth you can store. At times, it is all about statistics, and at times, about entrepreneurial foresight. The mega-theory that explains every aspect of economics is still elusive. We all are sorcerer's apprentices when it comes to economics. Almost every science impacts economics. But more importantly, economics impacts every science. And thus it is the machine that runs the world.

This book is a layman's user manual for this machine in which each of us is involved in some way. How does it impacts our lives? How to save and in what form? Where to invest and when? How to manage a business effectively? If this book has helped you in some way to answer any of these queries, even partially, I would consider that it has served its purpose. The book hopes that the reader gets a basic grasp of how the machine works and how to benefit from it. But those who want to master and understand it would be required to put a bit more effort. There is a vast body of knowledge, practical and theoretical, on the streets and in libraries that would help one master it. One has to keep looking for it and keep gathering this knowledge. I leave you with this one thought and, of course, with approximately 20 chapters this book is divided into.

Reading Resources

Macro Economics:

1. 'The End of Alchemy: Money, Banking and the Future of the Global Economy' by Mervyn King
2. 'The Ascent of Money: A Financial History of the World' by Niall Ferguson
3. 'Lords of Finance: The Bankers Who Broke the World' by Liaquat Ahamed

Finance and Investment:

4. 'Financial Intelligence for Entrepreneurs' by Karen Berman and Joe Knight
5. 'Intelligent Investor' by Ben Graham
6. 'How Finance Works – The HBR Guide to Thinking Smart About Numbers' by Mihir A. Desai
7. 'One Up on Wall Street' by Peter Lynch

Entrepreneurship and Business Biographies:

8. 'The Lean Startup' by Eric Ries
9. 'Zero to One' by Peter Thiel
10. 'Shoe Dog' by Phil Knight
11. 'Losing My Virginity' by Richard Branson

Part – II: Business Management, Finance and Company Operations

12. 'Made in America' by Sam Walton
13. 'I Too Had a Dream' by Verghese Kurien
14. 'The Ride of a Lifetime' by Robert Iger

Mergers, Acquisitions and Company Bios:

15. 'Smartest Guys in the Room' by Bethany McLean and Peter Elkind
16. 'Cold Steel' by Tim Bouquet and Byron Ousey

Strategy and Business Management

17. 'Innovators Dilemma' by Clayton Christensen
18. 'Only Paranoid Survive' by Andrew Grove
19. 'Good to Great: Why Some Companies Make The Lead and Others Don't' by Jim Collins

Manufacturing and Operations

20. 'The Goal' by Eliyahu Goldratt
21. 'The Machine that Changed the World' by Daniel Roos et al.
22. 'The Box' by Marc Levinson

Business Turnarounds:

23. 'From Worst to First' by Gordon Bethune

References

Preface:

1. Liaquat Ahamed, "Lords of Finance: The Bankers Who Broke the World", p: 504

Chapter 1:

1. Neil Borate, "How the top 5 cryptocurrencies fared in 2020", Live Mint, https://www.livemint.com/money/personal-finance/how-the-top-5-cryptocurrencies-fared-in-2020-11608292666156.html
2. BitCoin. Org, Available at https://bitcoin.org/en/faq#how-are-bitcoins-created
3. Live Mint, "Bitcoin to become legal currency in this country from September. How will it be used?", Available at https://www.livemint.com/market/cryptocurrency/bitcoin-to-become-legal-currency-in-this-country-from-september-how-will-it-be-used-11624589708811.html
4. King, M, 2016, "The End of Alchemy: Money, Banking and the Future of the Global Economy", p 180

Chapter 2:

1. Thomas Piketty, 2020, "Capital and Ideology", p 695
2. Thomas Piketty, 2020, "Capital and Ideology", p 657

Part – II: Business Management, Finance and Company Operations

Chapter 3:

1. King, M,2016, "The End of Alchemy: Money, Banking and the Future of the Global Economy", p 67
2. Niall Ferguson, "The Ascent of Money: A Financial History of the World", p106

Chapter 4:

1. Raghuram Rajan,2011, "Fault Lines", p 113

Chapter 5:

1. Tom Butler-Bowdon, 2017,"50 Economics Classics", p 295
2. Josephson, M, 1962, "The Robber Barons", page 47

Chapter 6:

1. Henry Hazlitt, "Economics in one Lesson", p75

Chapter 7:

1. Appelbaum. B, The Economists' Hour, p 23
2. Appelbaum. B, The Economists' Hour, p 172

Chapter 8:

1. https://scholarworks.umass.edu/cgi/viewcontent.cgi?article=1101&context=peri_workingpapers#:~:text=The%20Human%20Development%20Index%2C%20or,capita)%20(Sen%201985).
2. http://www.hdr.undp.org/en/content/assessing-human-development
3. https://www.weforum.org/agenda/2018/01/how-to-do-business-with-doughnuts/
4. Lawrence Burns, "Autonomy", p 166

5. https://storage.googleapis.com/waymo-uploads/files/documents/safety/2021-08-waymo-safety-report.pdf
6. https://www.transportenvironment.org/sites/te/files/downloads/T%26E%E2%80%99s%20EV%20life%20cycle%20analysis%20LCA.pdf
7. Rajan R., 2020, "The Third Pillar", pg 159
8. Harford, T, 2013, "The Under Cover Economist", pg 149
9. Rajan R., 2020, "The Third Pillar", pg 202
10. https://www.fda.gov/media/130883/download
11. Clayton Christensen, "The Innovator's Dilemma: When new technologies cause great firms to fail", Chapter 9, Loc: 3596.
12. Michael Munger, https://www.econtalk.org/michael-munger-on-sharing-transaction-costs-and-tomorrow-3-0/#:~:text=Michael%20Munger%20on%20Sharing%2C%20Transaction%20Costs%2C%20and%20Tomorrow%203.0,-Oct%2029%202018&text=Economist%20and%20author%20Michael%20Munger,how%20technology%20lowers%20transactions%20costs.
13. Rajan R., 2020, "The Third Pillar", p 189
14. Rajan R., 2020, "The Third Pillar", p 204
15. Ibid
16. Matt Ridley, "The Rational Optimist: How Prosperity Evolves", p 5
17. Simon Sinek, "Start With Why", p 88

Chapter 9:

1. Liaquat Ahamed, "Lords of Finance: The Bankers Who Broke the World", p: 497

2. Tom Butler-Bowdon, 2017,"50 Economics Classics", p 295
3. Niall Ferguson, "Ascent of Money: A Financial History of World", p 7
4. Brian McCullough, 2018, "A revealing look at the dot-com bubble of 2000 – and how it shapes our lives today", Available at: https://ideas.ted.com/an-eye-opening-look-at-the-dot-com-bubble-of-2000-and-how-it-shapes-our-lives-today/
5. Raghuram Rajan,2011, "Fault Lines", p 95
6. Raghuram Rajan,2011, "Fault Lines", p 97
7. Sanjaya Baru, 1991: How P. V. Narasimha Rao Made History, Chapter 2, Kindle Location: 607
8. Sanjaya Baru, 1991: How P. V. Narasimha Rao Made History, Chapter 2, Kindle Location: 1188
9. Sanjaya Baru, 1991: How P. V. Narasimha Rao Made History, p 78
10. Ibid
11. Sanjaya Baru, 1991: How P. V. Narasimha Rao Made History, p 80
12. Sanjaya Baru, 1991: How P. V. Narasimha Rao Made History, p 81
13. Sanjaya Baru, 1991: How P. V. Narasimha Rao Made History, p 85
14. Sanjaya Baru, 1991: How P. V. Narasimha Rao Made History, p 95
15. Liaquat Ahamed, "Lords of Finance: The Bankers Who Broke the World", p: 497
16. Liaquat Ahamed, "Lords of Finance: The Bankers Who Broke the World", p: 378
17. Liaquat Ahamed, "Lords of Finance: The Bankers Who Broke the World", p: 342

References

Chapter 13:

1. Hans Rosling, 2018, Factfulness, p 209

Chapter 16:

1. https://papers.ssrn.com/sol3/papers.cfm?abstract_id=837405

www.ingramcontent.com/pod-product-compliance
Lightning Source LLC
Chambersburg PA
CBHW020909180526
45163CB00007B/2682